DISCIPLESHIP

Pass It On!

Gary Beisheim

ISBN 979-8-88832-870-5 (paperback)
ISBN 979-8-88832-871-2 (digital)

Copyright © 2023 by Gary Beisheim

All rights reserved. No part of this publication may be reproduced, distributed, or transmitted in any form or by any means, including photocopying, recording, or other electronic or mechanical methods without the prior written permission of the publisher. For permission requests, solicit the publisher via the address below.

Christian Faith Publishing
832 Park Avenue
Meadville, PA 16335
www.christianfaithpublishing.com

Printed in the United States of America

Dedication

This book is first and foremost dedicated to Christ—who took my place on the cross and died—for me. Now, even though I had let Him into my heart, I walked away from Him for a while, and yet, MUCH like the story of the prodigal son, He stood there, and as I came back to Him, He stood there and welcomed me back with open arms. That love continues to motivate and propels me to stay with Him and get to know Him better.

Next, I dedicate this book to my wife who has kept encouraging me, discussing it with me, and just stayed by my side or in my room in ER so many times. She has clarified and simplified so many of my thoughts. I just wish I had written down so many of the times she has had God's quiet voice in this and life in general.

She is such a good wife. Proverbs 31 kind of captures it for me:

> A good wife who can find? She is far more
> precious that than jewels. (Prov 31:10 RSV)

Lastly, I want to thank and dedicate this book to all the guys who have trained me, encouraged me, and rebuked me (!) along the way. They have kept that fire burning in me and have in total brought me to this point in my life: all in!

Contents

Let's Get Some Things Straight between Us..................................1
   Let's Understand This Thing Called Sin 1
   Let's Understand "The Jesus I Know" 5
   Bonus Coverage...9
   Let's Understand Who Gets the Credit 10

My Christian Life in a Nutshell..12
   Childhood Memories of God (1950–1969) 12
   My Conversion and the Discipling Process Begins
      1970–1971...12
   The Lean Years (1972–1988) 17
   Prodigal Son Returns—Several Times! (1969–1990)............18
   Questions 20
   The Now (1991–2022) 21
   Jesus's Commands and Marching Orders Decoded 22

**Let's First Understand What Is Meant by the Word
   "Disciple"**..24
   Historical Use of the Word "Disciple" 29
   Another Source for the Definition of "Disciple" 31
   "Disciple" As Jesus Used It..32
   Jesus Talks About What It Is To Be A Disciple 34
   Are All of Us Called to Be Disciples..35

Do We Really Make Disciples? 37
    Is This Concept—And This Book—Just Meant for Men?.....39
    Does This Place a Burden on Everyone Who Is
        Discipling Another?...40
    What Can We Learn from Some Misguided Ministries? 42
    Three Things We Can Do to Make Godly Decisions............43
    Summary on the Words "Disciple" and "Making" Disciples 44
    Is This a Practical Study of Discipling or Is This an
        Intellectual Study of Jesus's Methods 45
    Examples of Discipling Programs in Today's Churches..........47
    Pay It Forward 50
    Making Disciples Is Not Meant for Everyone 55
    Encouragement 55
    Origins of the Walk with God 56

Jesus's Commands Boil Down to Only Two Commands............59
    Love God..59
        1) What does the Word of God say "discipline" is?.........60
        2) Loving God vs. Obedience..62
    How Do We Actually Love One Another? 65
    Question 66

Jesus's Last Marching Orders (Matthew 28:19–20) 68
    "Go" 68
    "Therefore" 71
    So How Do We Make Sense of All This? 72
    "Make Disciples" 75
    Biblical Examples of Use of the Word "Disciple" 80
    "Of All Nations" 84
    "Baptizing Them"...87
    "Teaching Them" 89
        The wheel 92
        The spokes..92

- 1. Reading the Bible 96
- 2. Studying the Bible 98
- 3. Study books of the Bible 100
- 4. Topical studies 100
- 5. Quiet times / devotionals 102
  - Get quiet 103
- The Word of God 104
- Write It Down! 106
  - "The Daily Kairos Journal" 108
  - 6. Meditating on His Word 109
  - 7. Commit His Words to your memory 111
  - 8. What gives us the right to pray? 115
  - 9. How should we pray? 116
  - 10. ACTS acronym 119
    - • A—Adoration 120
    - • C—Confession 121
    - • T—Thanksgiving 121
    - • S—Supplication (Requests) 122
  - 11. Prayer lists 123
  - 12. Additional thoughts and principles to be learned and passed on 124
  - 13. What prayer is not 125
- "To Observe" 126
  - "Just a walk in the park!" 126
- "All That I Have 'Commanded' You" 127
- "And lo, I am with you always, to the close of the age" 129

A Call to Action 131

Audience 133

BONUS: Excerpts from the Practice of the Presence of God......135
    1. Conversations..136
    2. Letters...139

Resources / References / Recommended Readings...................143
    Sources..143
    Discipleship...144
    Men's Issues..145
    Knowing the Will of God for Your Life 146
    Reference...146
    Additional Recommended Reading 147
    Small Group Studies..148

Let's Get Some Things Straight between Us

Let's Understand This Thing Called SIN

Okay, before we begin, let's see where each of you is coming from.

First question: has anyone reading this book not sinned?

Hmmm...

Well, if you have never sinned, <u>Welcome Back, Jesus!</u>

Come on out to Seattle. I'm dying to meet you face-to-face!

If you have ever sinned, well then, we all—ALL—start from a level playing field. Yep, we've all sinned—even the Pope—even Billy Graham did it too!

Think of the best, most loving, and/or gracious, forgiving human being you have EVER met, and yet, they did it—that sin thing. Actually, most of us have gotten really good at this sinning thing.

Okay, we really ARE on the same level on the playing field.

However, there IS hope. It is in the person of Christ

When Jesus was dying on the cross, He uttered these words to a man, a convicted thief who spoke up, rebuked the other criminal being hung, and told him, "This man has done nothing wrong," and Jesus said to him: "Truly I say to you, today you will be with me in Paradise" (Luke 23:43 RSV).

This all does not discourage me; in fact, it generously encourages me that everyone is redeemable!

Now comes the beautiful part, and it's personal—it's for you.

God sent His Son who knows what you did, and <u>just</u> before you are to be put on a cross and killed, Jesus steps in and takes your place. You were supposed to die, but Jesus, this guy you don't even know and whom you have never met, pays the price for you and dies.

THEN, He conquers death, comes back to life, goes to heaven, and get this (after actually dying for you): invites you to join Him with His family and live eternally with Him in joy AND share all that He has. YOU are heirs to His kingdom; He has prepared a place for you—a home.

I am sorry, but I get tears in my eyes every time I recount this amazing story. That's what the word "grace" is all about; we deserved death, and He (freely!) gives us life. There is no greater love than this.

This is what propels and is the basis for this book; this unfathomable love—for me, for you.

The utterly amazing thing to me is it's a totally free gift!

I mean it's like going to a party and being given an unexpected gift, although you didn't bring one and you didn't have to pay to get in!

If you acknowledge the work of Jesus Christ for you (!) and accept Him, in time, you will understand more and more, and yet, we will never understand it all. Once you grasp this, you can help others understand the depth of this love.

People who have not accepted Christ into their hearts do not feel like they are the lost. They are not wandering; they may or may not even be seekers, i.e., people who are seeking the truth. You may be in THIS boat.

I clearly remember the verse that brought me to Christ: Rev 3:20, "Behold I stand at the door and knock; if anyone hears my voice and opens the door, I will come in to him and eat with him, and he with me."

The keys here are:

1. God's always knocking. Always.
2. We—you—must open the door.

DISCIPLESHIP

I think many—who do not know Christ—are not hearing and may not be listening.

They may feel, "Life is good!"—as is.

They may feel like, "Okay, I go to church. That's good enough! I don't have to go deeper than that. My life and family and job are okay. I don't want to mess that up." You may be in THIS boat: you know OF Christ, but you stop there.

Remember, we ALL are on the same level, but this book won't make a lot of sense if you haven't confronted that primary issue of "Okay, God, I get that I am a sinner, and I want you to come into my life—however that looks, whatever changes that might mean."

This book comes toward following Jesus in your own life and how to do that AND out of gratitude (!), helping another guy follow and model Jesus in their life. This is the whole book in a nutshell.

Okay, given this common ground, this book seeks to answer a couple of simple questions:

1. What IS a disciple? And are we all called to BE disciples? (The answer is not what you think or have been told and is not quite that simple!)
2. What does God really require of us? I.e., what did Jesus actually command us to do?
3. Is it imperative that we pass on to other what we have observed, learned, and/or inculcated? If so, how do we do that / what does it look like in today's world?
4. What are some ways we can develop a closer—a more friend-like relationship—with Christ?

This book asks and tackles the tough questions, knowing full well that this might fly in the face of the church's opinion and use of the command to make disciples:

- What did Jesus really mean when He said, "Go and make disciples…teaching them to observe all I COMMANDED you."

DISCIPLESHIP

- Following that, has the CHURCH watered it down and implemented something not even resembling Jesus's true instruction?
- If Jesus commanded us to "love God," then, how do we do this / what does it look like lived out? Do we spend most of our time loving God or just on Sundays?
- Following that command, what do the three points of emphasis mean for our daily lives when Jesus said, "<u>With all your heart, with all your soul and with all your mind</u>"?
- One version translates Jesus's words in His second command as "Love ONE ANOTHER"; another version translates that as "Love YOUR NEIGHBOR," which is right, and again, how do we do this / what does it look like lived out? That begs the question, "Do we really have to 'love' THAT person?" You know, the one that is unlovable, where there is seemingly no good in that person.
- Why do almost all churches stop in discipling with making a person into a Disciple and not emphasize this is meant to be passed on? Do we hand them a Bible and then tell them lovingly, "Good luck"? My contention is, all people who believe need someone to come alongside them and help them. Whether you just became a believer, trusting God with your eternity or someone who has gone to church for fifty or more years, we ALL need an encourager, a teacher, a model we can emulate.
- What are the elements that a discipler must be and then pass on and then get passed on and on? With that comes the question: how do you make sure the knowledge is correct and not watered down?

Now, do you want to know the answers to these questions?

If not, stop reading now and read the questions posed again before going any further exploring and considering the answers to the questions that I posed.

The answers might give a framework for the book and can be on your mind to try and find answers in this book to those questions that matter to YOU.

Good luck!

Let's Understand "The Jesus I Know"

So where am I coming from?

Good question!

Although naturally I have never seen Jesus, I believe I've seen bits of evidence of Jesus in various people I've met over the years. Although I've (obviously) never had the chance to sit down with Jesus and talk about stuff, I have seen reflections of Him in some specific people I have had the privilege of getting to know. In this book, you will read of some of those glimpses I have had of His face, His heart! It's like the mirror disco ball that used to hang in the middle of a dance hall that would reflect light shining on it: you can't see the whole light—only a tiny piece of it.

The Jesus I know is humble and doesn't require/demand a lot from us; He wanted Himself to be a place of rest and a life with Him that did not demand a heavy yoke or workload! I know this statement may offend a lot of authors and theologians—who <u>demand</u> a 100 percent commitment, a life full of things we MUST do.

We make a 100 percent commitment—ONLY out of a realization of what He sacrificed for us—and thus we act and live from a sense or attitude of gratitude—not out of obligation or a feeling, no matter how deeply seated—that we could live lives holy enough to make up for or pay for what He freely gave us.

Read carefully for yourselves to what the Master, Jesus, said about himself (Matt 11:28–29 RSV):

> <u>Come to me</u>, all who labor and are heavy laden, and I will give you **rest**.
> Take my yoke upon you, and learn from me; for **<u>I am gentle and lowly in heart,</u>** and you

> will find rest for your souls. For my yoke is easy, and my burden is light.

Those words were from Jesus.
Does that sound like a hard taskmaster? No!
Does this sound like a demanding guy? No!
Does this relationship with Him sound like a lot of work? No!
Do you sometimes feel overburdened or lost? He says simply, "Come to me."

I have felt that way—that it became a set of gotta-do's: morning devotionals—EVERY morning—Bible verse memory and meditation, and don't forget to pray EVERY single night! I have come to know Jesus / God as a VERY patient and loving Father and Friend.

Now this may fly in the face of contradiction to what the Apostles wrote following Jesus's departure.

In Paul's letter to the church in Philippi, he wrote, "Therefore, my beloved, as you have always obeyed, so now, not only as in my presence but much more in my absence, <u>work out your own salvation</u> with fear and trembling, for God is at work in you, both to will and to work for His good" (Phil 2:12–13 RSV).

A couple of things:

- It SOUNDS as though it is not a free gift that we need to work for salvation.
    - o In context, Paul exhorts us in the preceding verses, "That at the name of Jesus every knee should bow, in heaven and earth and under the earth, and every tongue confess that Jesus Christ is Lord. To the glory of God the Father" (Phil 2:10–11 RSV). I think Paul is reminding us: realize whom you are in relationship with! That's why he starts off with "Therefore."
    - o Paul states it clearly: it is God working IN you; you do NOT get there (to heaven) because of your "good works." It's humbling, but Paul reminds us GOD is at work in us—for His purpose—as HE wills. We do very little.

James writes in James 2:18, "But some will say, 'You have faith and I have works.' Show me your faith apart from your works, and I by my works will show you my faith."

- In this section, James is simply saying faith and resulting works are interconnected. If you have faith, works will follow, and they work together. It's not faith alone; your faith will be shown in your works. In nonreligious speak: if you grow closer to Christ, you won't be able to help it, you will feel the joy, and that joy will overflow into obedience to His leading and love or what they call good works.

Others quote Abraham's obedience as being considered as salvation (righteousness). Thank GOD for Christ! In Abraham's day, he didn't have the Christ to impute TO him righteousness. We now have the work of Christ to give us righteousness, i.e., we can now stand before God BECAUSE of Christ, NOT because of anything we do or did,

This is all put out there ONLY to help you understand the need for a discipler to help you work through these (and other) seeming contradictions!

This (again) is not a scholarly work on faith vs. works; it never was intended to be. It IS about encouraging you, as a disciple, that you too need someone to discuss this with. Further, your guys, your disciples, will want to and need to work through this concept!

Make sense?

This will become more readily apparent as you continue reading the book, but these things you do (reading, prayer, study, devotionals) should not become mere tasks or things to be checked off a list; however, it is useful that they become habits, but they should never become something you HAVE TO do.

And read this from Matthew 20:28 (RSV), <u>*"Even as the Son of man came **not** to be served but to serve and to give His life as a ransom for many."*</u>

Does this guy sound like a heavy-handed boss? He could have... He chose not to.

Okay, here is the logic that will pervade this book; *stay with me on this:*

The last part of the Matthew 20:28 (quoted above) is not trivial and is not an afterthought**; it is everything**!

Follow the logic concepts that follows from that little phrase: *"And to give His life as a ransom for many."*

1. First, Jesus commanded us to **love one another** (Matt 22:37–40 NIV): *"Jesus replied (to the Pharisees) Love the Lord your God with all your heart and with all your soul and with all your mind. This is the first and greatest Commandment. And the second is like it.* **Love your neighbor as yourself.** *All the Law and prophets hang on these two commandments."*
2. THEN Jesus is quoted as having said (John 15:13 NIV): *"Greater love has no one; to lay down one's life for one's friends."*
3. Then, as you read above, Jesus died—willingly—to ransom or pay the price for our sins. This is a sacrificial gift, one that Jesus gave his life for. That kind of love still freaks me out.
4. Okay, guys, this last one is for you (Eph 5:25 and 29): *"Husbands **love your wives, just as Christ loved the church and gave Himself up for her**… In this same way, husbands ought to love their wives as their own bodies. He who loves his wife loves himself."*

So Christ gave himself up for the church. He gave up His life—quite literally—(i.e., He died for His bride, the church).

I speak to guys, as I am a guy!

(Ladies, you have your own burden and accountability.)

Guys, do you get it?

- Jesus told us to "love one another."
- Then Jesus tells us how **and to what extent!**

We must (sacrificially) give up our thoughts, wants, our lives—for our wife!

DISCIPLESHIP

The burden is really on us, Guys!
That's not fun to hear, but it can be life-changing!

Bonus Coverage

Ponder this one for a moment:

Jesus IS God and WAS God. Should we then think that God the Father is any different? Think about it.

Jesus said He came to serve, so why do we imagine that God the Father chooses to sit high up on His throne and we are all His little peons.

No, I think God the Father cares as much for us, wants to serve each of us, just as Jesus did!

This guy came into life, came into OUR world in a farm animals' stable and spent his first night on earth in an animal's feeding trough!

This guy made His TRIUMPHANT entrance back into Jerusalem riding on a (borrowed) donkey (Ref: Matt 21).

Is this the Jesus YOU know?

Do YOU feel that Christ loves YOU that much?

So Jesus loves us, but what DID Jesus expect of us or command?

Jesus only **commanded** us to do two things, and this book will explore them both in depth (see Matt 22:34–40):

1. Love God with all your heart, soul, and mind, and
2. Love one another.

That's it. (We are going to spend some time in this book on these two things!)

I approach God daily, not because it's on a checklist, but because I want to. I find comfort in Him ("I will be with you ALWAYS"), I find joy in praising Him, I sometimes just sit or stand in awe of Him, just trying to grasp how big God is, and yet how, somehow, Jesus cares for and died for little old me! For a moment, make this personal: Jesus died <u>for just you</u>.

When we read "he died for all sins," it is kind of impersonal, but when you meet with Him and get to know Him, you too can grasp that Jesus was willing to die for just you. You (and I!) deserved it—death—and He took our place and died for little old you.

I hope like heck this concept can touch your heart so you can know that Jesus wants more than anything to come down and talk to and listen to you and me. My hope is that you can grasp it—maybe now for the first time—and that, in time, you will be able to pass this on to your guys!

I hope you will pause here and let this personal sacrifice sink in: that Jesus gave his life for you as real and He did it for you. That death was not "Oh, He fell asleep and died of suffocation." It hurt; it killed Him. But He was willing to do it for you and me! Man, that sacrifice really gets me.

Little additional benny (benefit): Jesus rose from the dead! This means, we are not only spared death (which we deserved for our sins), but He rose, which means we get life with Him for eternity! That life is gonna be with the same, humble guy! It's not going to be drudgery or listening to stale organ music; think of your happiest moment ever and multiply that by say one million times and that will not approach this joy we will experience.

Let's Understand Who Gets the Credit

Another thing that needs to be clear at the outset: these are not my words: all glory goes to God. I am just a guy, just like you, but God brought a man into my life that introduced or directed me to Jesus and then helped me along the way!

I wish there were a way to express the gratitude I feel for that happening! THAT is why for the past fifty-plus years, I have tried to help come alongside or disciple other men to pass it on. That's what this book is about.

There have been so many times during the writing of this book where I have not felt worthy to write it. However, and this may sound presumptuous of me, but I have felt God has told me, THIS needs to be "passed on" to others. During that time, I have had a couple of pastors, mentors, coaches tell me to continue. "Just write the book!" one exclaimed!

DISCIPLESHIP

Each time I have sat down to write this down, almost without exception, I have started, before hitting a single key, asking God to "Open my eyes, Lord, I want to see Jesus!" If it is valuable, the words are from God, not me.

If ANY of this writing helps even ONE other person or inspires them to draw nearer to God or encourages or spurs them on to help one other person, then the words are from God and He gets the credit and the glory from it.

I may duplicate this story later in the book, so I apologize, but recently, I wrote to a former pastor and mentor, saying I was not seeing fruit from my discipleship ministry, and his reply will stay in my mind forever. He replied simply, **"Don't worry about it. God does the counting. Just write the book."**

In writing this, I have tried to heed the advice given in Psalm 46:10, "Be still and know that I am God." Recently, I learned that this really has a different meaning than I have thought for years! The word "still" comes from the Hebrew word, "rapa," meaning "surrender, let go, drop what you are holding on to so tightly."

To know God means to acknowledge or see with our eyes God's impact on our lives and to trust HIM.

If there is any good in this book, if anything comes from this book, as in it helps another Christian get closer to God, then:

a. God should get all the glory from it (I will explain what I mean), and
b. It was worth the years it took to develop me and this work to a point of some clarity.

I believe every single time I sat down to write what's been passed on to me, I asked for His help. I asked for His words, not mine. So if this work is true and helps even that one guy, it's His words, not mine, and on the other hand, if it gathers great criticism, then it's my word.

My Christian Life in a Nutshell

Childhood Memories of God (1950–1969)

As probably happened to many of you, I grew up in a family that went to church, so I grew up going to church. However, there was no relationship with God—no real knowledge of what Christ had done for me. I grew up going to a Lutheran Church in Colorado. I memorized the entire Lutheran Catechism and was confirmed. It was pastored by an amazing guy, Ivan Anderson. Even then, I saw in this man some things of Christ that I thought, *I'd like to be more like that!* More loving. On a hike near the Flat Irons in Boulder, I fell. Pastor Anderson picked me up in his arms and carried me all the way down the trail to our car. That's giving love.

My Conversion and the Discipling Process Begins 1970–1971

The next contact with God came when I was in the military at Laredo (Texas) Air Force Base. One afternoon, a guy came knocking at my door, and I opened it and talked with him for a while and he invited me to church, a Bible study, and a trip to San Antonio to hear a prominent guy, Bob Lewis (who was then a regional director for the Navigators Organization). I don't remember going to church with Mike nor any Bible studies, but I did go with him to San Antonio.

DISCIPLESHIP

In Bob Lewis's living room, a group of us guys sat and stood around as Bob opened his Bible, as it just kind of opened up naturally like a book that had been used a lot.

I only remember one verse from that evening, and it has stayed with me for fifty years now (Rev 3:20): *"Behold I stand at the door and knock; if anyone hears my voice and opens the door, I will come into him and eat with him, and he with me."*

Later that evening, as I was going to sleep in a sleeping bag on the floor with some other guys in Bob Lewis's basement, I distinctly remember thinking, *I had never invited Jesus into my heart, into my life*—and I invited Christ in right there. I slept well that night, totally at peace.

The guy who invited me to San Antonio started spending more and more time with me, getting to know each other, but more importantly, getting to know this Christ character.

- We started having what we called quiet times (or QTs); some call it morning devotionals. Sometimes, we'd meet in his car, sometimes (my favorite times!) at the lake just outside the AFB walls, reading the Bible, discussing what it meant to each of us, writing down a takeaway thing that impacted us—all as the sun came up over the horizon. Totally great times. (I will discuss how you can have your own quiet times later in the book.)
- We had fun together as well! He had a small sailing boat, no motor, and we'd take it out to that lake, and he'd take us out for a sail. A funny aside: I made the mistake one time, thinking I KNEW how to sail. Wrong! This guy let me have the till and try to get us back to shore. He didn't say a word, as I made mistake after mistake and eventually beached the sailboat. At which time, he said famously, "A boat can have only one captain"; as I hopped out of the boat, I grabbed the rope at the front end of the boat (I think they call it the bow, right? LOL.), and I towed it back to where we could put it on the trailer. Lesson learned. Funny now, not then. I do miss Mike now.

DISCIPLESHIP

- The Navigators—of which I later learned Bob Lewis was a regional director or something big—would have periodically got together the guys from Nav. Ministries at various army and air force bases in Texas. On one occasion, we had one at Laredo AFB. Several significant things happened at the one held at Laredo AFB:
    o A baseball game. This wasn't any ordinary softball game; the pitcher was Bob Lewis and the ump was the Laredo AFB Nav Ministry guy, Charles Hardie. The two of them would exchange barbs as each disagreed with the other's calls or comments. This was different though; they wouldn't swear. They'd use and throw out and quote memorized scripture at each other. It was hilarious! I don't remember a single verse they threw at each other, but remember, the other guy would quickly come back with his own scripture barb.
    o Teaching the Wheel to other guys. I will describe the wheel later in the book, but it's four aspects of the Christian life that, like spokes on a wheel, need to be in some sort of balance with Christ as the Hub. I got to teach this; it was a step toward maturity in faith.
- I do remember "my discipler" asking me one time, "Gar, do you want help or do you want training?" I chose training. He trained me. Eventually, I got invited to live in the home with the Laredo AFB Navs, Charles and Phyllis Hardie, for close-in training and seeing how real couples interact and raise kids. Great time. Later, I went off to Airborne Training at Fort Benning in Georgia, and later, Charles and Phyllis went off to Taiwan for thirteen years as missionaries and then nineteen years in Siberia. We would meet up again. I will tell you about that reunion later.
- I began discipling other guys at Laredo AFB: Doug, Dan, Jim, Joe, Steve. It was common practice (I guess!) in Nav Ministries to keep Journals on the progress of "your guys." For some reason, I guess because I liked my guys so much, I have kept the actual journals I had on each guy. On the

next page, I have blacked out the name of the record of work with one guy, but included in this book is a copy of the actual record I kept of discipling one guy fifty years ago.

The "verse card" I had then and still have even today was 1 Thessalonians 2:8, *"Because we loved you, it was a JOY to us to give you not only the gospel, but, our very hearts so dear did you become to us"* (emphasis added).

This attitude kind of pervaded all my actions and life with these guys and still does today to ALL the guys I have discipled.

Do you know something? I don't know where any of these five guys are now, what their lives have been like, or whether and how much my life and discipling impacted the lives of guys. Where did they invest their lives? Did they pour out THEIR lives into other men? Hmmm.

Someday, I will know. I will meet them when I see and meet with Jesus. Someday. They are my "riches stored in heaven."

This will become clearer to you when I talk about YOU making disciples especially when you are discipling more than one guy.

I had a way of tracking things, basics, of which I had shared:

o   (S) meant Shared,
o   (D) meant does, meaning, this person, on his own does the item, like read the Bible, which I marked as "D" or "T" for we did it together, etc.

DISCIPLESHIP

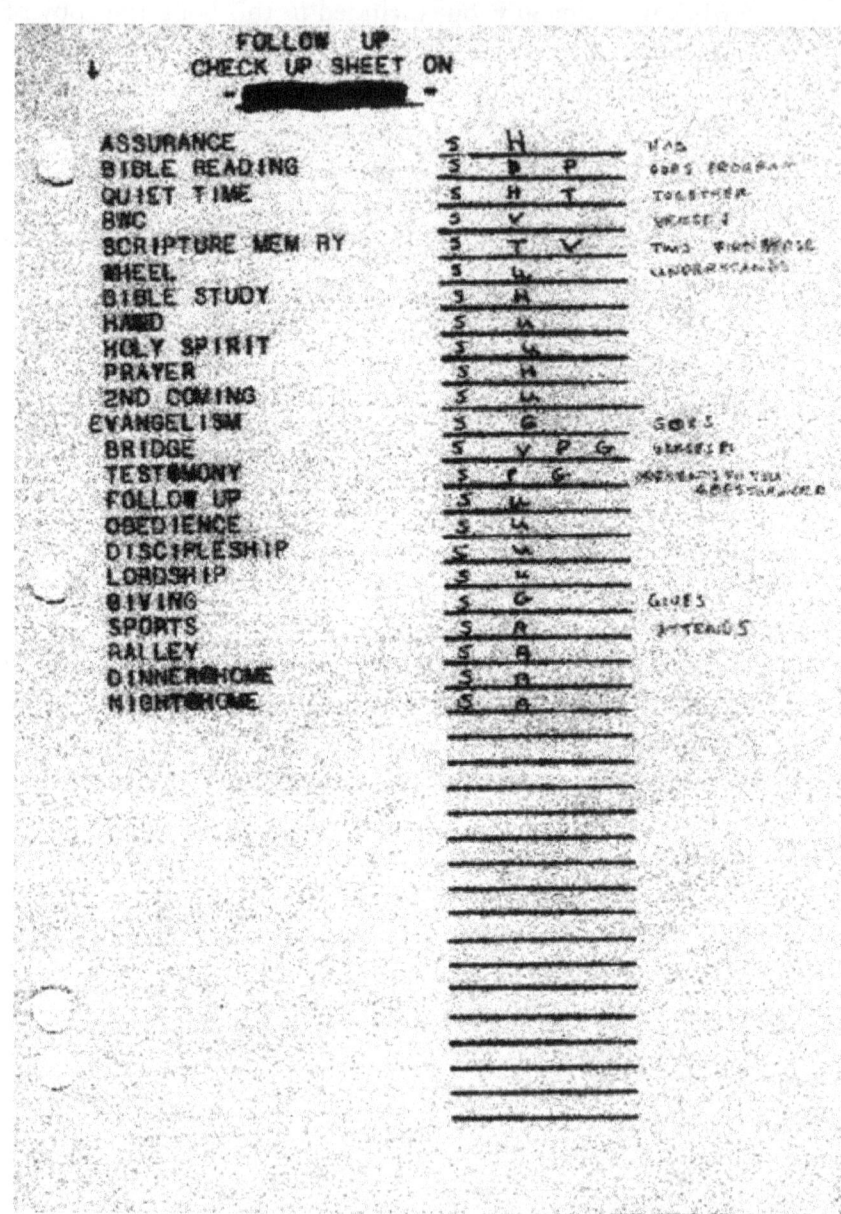

16

DISCIPLESHIP

The Lean Years (1972–1988)

When I left Laredo AFB and went first to airborne (parachute jumper) training in Fort Benning, Georgia, then later to serve at Howard AFB in Panama, I kind of turned my back on Jesus. Yes, I see it as amazing even now!

When I went to jump school, I did hold on to one promise of God, which my wife, Sue, had beautifully framed and has hung prominently in our home: *"But those who wait upon the Lord will renew, **they will mount up with wings like eagles, they will run and not grow weary, they will walk and not feint**"* (Is 40:31).

In jump school, we ran three miles practically every morning before breakfast, and I was upheld by this verse and by God and I got my "wings."

Walking away happened, and can happen today, quickly. I had no spiritual support or connection down in Panama. It was, and can be, easy to walk away. It's easy and can be something simple as finding a diversion: sports on TV or more free time. It's important to note, God did not walk away from me. I just forgot about Him for a while—about fifteen years as I recollect now. There was no going to church to even say, "Thanks!"

There were no quiet times with Christ, no prayer life, no time in the Word. Nothing!

There is something IMPORTANT to discuss here: being alone as a Christian. You don't have to be thousands of miles away—in Panama or Vietnam—to feel alone. You can walk in and out of a church for twenty years and not help or be helped or lifted up by another Christian. That, I think, is one of the big flaws in the Church today; there is no discipling going on! We all NEED someone to teach us (an Apostle Paul type figure) and for us to teach (as in Paul's young disciple, Timothy, a young pastor in Thessalonica) and a "Barnabas" type character, someone who is not enamored or impressed by us and importantly who keeps us accountable.

Don't be alone, or you too may, someday, just drift away from the church. This is hard, especially for introverts, where contact with others drains them of energy! Don't allow this to happen; take a step out of your comfort zone and seek out someone to come alongside you.

When I came out of the Air Force in 1972, I enrolled at URI, the University of Rhode Island. I do recall signing up for classes, and they had a booth—I believe it was Campus Crusade. I tried to make a connection there. I even remember asking (in a very awkward way!), "Hey, are we gonna go knock on the barracks doors?" (They are dorms, Gary, not barracks! LOL.) However, no one followed up. That's not to knock them; it's just mentioned to again emphasize how important this one-on-one connection is. Guys, you can perish without contact—real contact—with another Christian!

I was married in 1972, but that ended in divorce in (about) 1984 to 1985. We had a child, Karyn, and when she was just seven or so, she ended up moving with her mom to the Dallas, Texas, area. To be honest, my relationship with Karyn deteriorated from that point—till even now. My point here is not to dwell on things between Karyn and I; it is to realize that God wants marriages to work and to stay together.

Prodigal Son Returns—Several Times! (1969–1990)

After my divorce to Suzanne, I rented a room from and ended up marrying Sue on Christmas Eve 1988 who, at this writing, is still my godly, God-fearing wife!

In short, if you want to know what I think of my wife, read Proverbs 31:25–31! Okay, go ahead and read the whole Proverb 31! Like Proverbs 31:10, _"A good wife who can find? She is far more precious than jewels."_

In 1990, we had a son, a man whom I am and have always been so proud! Around that time, we decided, "We need to be going to church!"

I think Travis was the impetus that brought me back to God.

Do you know what? JUST like the Old Testament story of the Prodigal Son, God WARMLY welcomed me back to His open arms and gave me a BIG hug! There is a lesson I think in each of these chapters of my life, and this one some or many of you may relate: that no matter how long you have been away from Him or how far you have gone away from Him, no matter what you are engaged in now, God WILL welcome you back, just as He did me.

I come back realizing He died in place of me and then I kind of ignored Him. Geez, Gar! THEN He welcomes me back? THAT is unfathomable!

We found a church, a church plant, in Fremont, California. As I think about it, that was God. The pastor there—a humble man, a servant of God, who later would become a mentor to me as I started a men's ministry, as I led Bible studies, as we studied discipleship in Greg Ogden's classic thirty-week study. Now, to even mention this pastor's name here, I KNOW he would reply, "No, Gar, to GOD be the glory! God be glorified!" So I apologize, but this man reflected a part of this God I know, the loving part, the humility, the patience, the servant heart. I have admired you and tried to emulate or imitate you, **as you imitated Christ**.

At that church, I discipled one guy and then one other. The first guy and I were in the choir together (my "in tune days" LOL), and we got to talking, and both realized the church had no real men's ministry! It had golf outings and prayer breakfasts where no one prayed! So under the pastor's advice and consult, we started a men's ministry. We had Bible studies attended by about six to eight guys very regularly, with great interest.

One of those guys, now deceased, came alongside another guy and encouraged him in the faith. He and I are still FB friends, and I see from his posts; he is excitedly still in the faith!

One of the guys and I started having regular meetings over lunch at a Denny's in San Jose. That's notable because I was the big discipler, right? BMOC! (Big Man of Christ)! Well, here's an awakening for you, the teacher, can still learn! At one of our lunches, we always asked each other three questions (you may see this again in another part of the book!)

1. How is your walk with God?
2. How is your marriage?
3. Have you just lied to me?

DISCIPLESHIP

Well, in relaying all my work at my job as a controller, he had the AUDACITY (!) to tell me, "Gar, I think you are spending too much time at your job!" (I was pretty regularly working till 10:00 p.m. or so.)

At that moment, I actually wanted to get up and reach across the table and punch him! Really!

After a week (maybe longer! LOL), I finally realized he was telling the truth—the truth in love—and I changed my work and started spending more time at home!

Stuff like this, real stuff, can actually happen in a discipling relationship! It's not all one-sided.

Three of us in the Men's Ministry Group guys ended up going to a PK (Promise Keepers) gathering of about fifty thousand men in Anaheim, California. One of these guys ended up going with his wife on a mission to Africa! We formed bonds there that remain. Last year, two of us travelled to Cowboy Stadium in Dallas, Texas, to a Promise Keepers (PK) Event. Amazingly, catching up, with about ten years since we had seen each other, was almost instantaneous! He was still connected with God; it was joy that brought us both to tears.

There were two other guys coming out of an earlier PK Conference in the Oakland Coliseum that met with me each Saturday morning at about 6:30. Guys, that's EARLY, but they were faithful. We studied Greg Ogden's thirty-week course on discipleship. I do not know how they are doing these days, but do recall, in leading that study, to my failing, I did NOT feel the need to—and did not—emphasize to take it to the next generation (2 Tim 2:2).

During this time, my wife and I went through the Ogden course together as I discipled her. She later took that on to several other women, one of which has gone to lead studies in Lexington, Kentucky. I recall her and Sue doing the study together and then celebrating the completion over a meal and a good bottle of Chardonnay! Great times!

Questions

Is there a guy in your life right now you are pouring your life into and trying to reflect Christ to? Hmmm.

DISCIPLESHIP

Is there a guy in your life who is teaching you, walking by your side through your life?

You are never too old to start this process, always remembering it's God who brings the growth. (See 1 Corinthians 3:5–9.)

The Now (1991–2022)

Around September 2000, I bought a freight-forwarding company in Seattle. That obviously necessitated a search for a new church. Being a fully trained and certified public accountant, I had a chart wherein I evaluated each aspect of a church that was important to us (aspects like: Is it biblically based and sound? Is it centered around Christ? Is it uplifting?). But of course, a chart!

We had ratings on each church, such things as energy, adherence to the truth found in the Word of God, and then, naturally, I had weightings for each factor, coming up with a weighted score for each church. It was quite a search—almost thirty weeks?

Some of this is just personal, but we liked and wanted a praise band that brought energy to worship. In contrast, when we walked in and heard organ music, we'd look at each other, get up quickly, and exit.

Again, that's personal style—just as your relationship with God—will probably be quite different than ours.

In some churches, we found it was made up primarily of people older than dirt; we left.

In some churches, we found the focus was, in our judgment, in error (i.e., in one church, the walls were plastered with architectural drawings of the new building); we left.

We found biblical teaching and joy and energy in worship in a church in Redmond, Washington: Timberlake. We lived in Issaquah, Washington, so it was about a thirty-minute drive, but it was worth it. Since then, we moved to Des Moines, Washington, and we tried to find a comparable church locally but, ended up driving about forty-five minutes back to Timberlake in Redmond, Washington.

The notable thing here is even after our move to Des Moines, I found a guy in whom I felt a kindred heart and he emulated Christ in some ways I wanted to model, like his humility, his faithfulness, his servant heart, and his love for the study of the Bible. We continued to meet almost every week even when, with my health issues, it became somewhat difficult! He has knowledge of the Word; we actually met in one of the studies he conducted on one of the Gospels. He continues to lead studies, BUT also reaches out to help other guys, one who has moved, but he does stay in touch with him. He also is "working with" a guy who has gone on to lead Bible studies with other men.

Do you get a glimpse of how it can work in the real life of a man, just a man, not some perfect pastor? I also am just a guy, following Christ. I pray that God will bring me men that I can come alongside and help and emulate Christ for them. This process has changed; I no longer keep journals on each man. I just meet them where they are, wherever they are. Maybe I should go back to journals, so I don't miss a step in their process to becoming spiritually mature. I am praying about that as well!

Now that you have a glimpse of how I came to this point in time and how God has touched my heart through the years, the rest of the book is a (rather) simple guide to this Christian life and how you can help others.

Jesus's Commands and Marching Orders Decoded

It has become clear to me that the Christian life can be boiled down to just two instructions Jesus called commands.

1. Love God with all your heart and with all your soul and with all your strength, and
2. Love one another.

This book goes into great detail as to what I believe those two simple commands mean.

If you grasp that, THEN you can try to live out His last marching orders when Jesus said, "Therefore go and make disciples" (Matt 28:19–20).

DISCIPLESHIP

I have written about this a bit differently. As kind of a form of meditation, I have taken each part of that familiar quote and dwelt on the importance and meaning of each individual word or phrase.

Let's First Understand What Is Meant by the Word "Disciple"

Any book claiming to be about discipling (Christian mentoring or coaching) necessarily needs to begin with the true definition of a disciple.

In learning what Jesus intended by the phrase "*Make disciples,*" there is an obvious need to know and understand the word "disciple": what it meant then and why Jesus used that particular term in His last instructions.

- What did Jesus really command us to do?

Hint: Jesus did NOT say:

- "Go and build ten thousand buildings" or,
- "Go and just start a bunch of small groups."
    Jesus was more specific about what He wanted passed on, and it was specifically talking about the training of the individual, not just some general teaching as He would in addressing a crowd.
- What did He want us to be or do, and what commands did He want us to obey?
- Can we really live in today's world and live fully and as happily as God intended?
- Is this something we can learn and do and be?

- Can we duplicate or replicate that in another person's life? Can we, you and I, really be disciple makers?
- Do WE actually do the making of a disciple?

The answers to these questions should be prefaced with a clear understanding of the word, disciple.

The following provides the historic use of the term as well as the biblical basis for this definition. This book is practical above all else as a guide, not only in BEING a disciple, but **very importantly**, taking it to the next generation.

I recently read an article that put it in plain English.

The article is titled, "In the Dust of the Rabbi: Clarifying Discipleship for Faith Formation Today," by Edward Sri, STD in Issue #4.2 of *Catechetical Review*:

> In the first-century Jewish world of Jesus, being a disciple was all about one key word: *imitation*. When a disciple followed a rabbi, the goal wasn't merely to master the rabbi's teachings but also to imitate the way he lived: the way he prayed, studied, taught, served the poor, and lived out his relationship with God day-to-day. Jesus himself said when a disciple is fully trained, he "becomes **like** his teacher" (Lk 6:40). And when St. Paul formed disciples of his own, he exhorted them not just to remember his teachings, but also to follow his way of living: "Be imitators of me as I am of Christ" (1 Cor 11:1).
>
> Though the word disciple (*mathetes*) means "learner," biblical discipleship was very different from modern classroom learning. On a college campus, a professor might give lectures to students in a large hall; the students take notes, and they're examined on the material later in the semester. But there's usually not an ongoing personal relationship and sharing of life between

professor and student in the university setting today.

To follow a rabbi, however, meant living with the rabbi, sharing meals with him, praying with him, studying with him, and taking part in the rabbi's daily life. A rabbi's life was meant to be a living example of someone shaped by God's Word. Disciples, therefore, studied not just the text of Scripture but also the "text" of the rabbi's life.

This is why Jesus didn't simply ask his disciples to listen to his preaching in the synagogues. He said, "Come, follow me," and basically invited them on a three-year camping trip as they journeyed throughout Galilee together during his itinerant ministry. Think about that: day in and day out for three years living with Jesus! How much they would have been influenced by his example! They'd notice the way he woke up early to pray. They'd witness his compassion in helping the sick. They'd be struck by his pressing need to go out to the sinners, Gentiles, and outcasts. They'd also observe how he taught the crowds, debated his opponents, called people to repent, and offered them mercy. Much of Jesus's way of living would have rubbed off on his disciples.

So if we're going to live as disciples of Jesus today, we must aim for a lot more than believing a set of doctrines and following the rules of our faith. All that, of course, is essential, but we must go deeper and consider what's happening interiorly: are we moving closer to Christ, encountering him anew each day?

Discipleship is something intensely dynamic. It implies movement and transformation as the disciple deepens his friendship with Christ and becomes ever more like him.

DISCIPLESHIP

According to one ancient Jewish saying, if you encounter a rabbi, you should "cover yourself in the dust of his feet and drink in his words thirstily." This expression likely draws on a well-known sight for ancient Jews: disciples were known for walking behind their rabbi, following him so closely that they would become covered with the dust kicked up from his sandals. This would have been a powerful image for what should happen in the disciple's life spiritually. Disciples were expected to follow their rabbi so closely that it's as if they would be covered with their master's way of thinking, living, and acting.

Thousands of years later, we're called to do the same. Though we walk on roads of pavement and not dust, we are still called to be disciples—to follow our Rabbi Jesus Christ so closely that we are covered with his life, changed, and made new.

In Acts 2:42, the Bible underscores four practices that marked the earliest disciples of Jesus. We can think of these as four key habits of a disciple. The disciples in the early Church devoted themselves to:

1. The teaching of the apostles
2. Fellowship
3. The breaking of bread
4. Prayers…

St. Paul said to the Christian disciples in Thessalonica, "We gave you not only the Gospel, but our very selves…" (1 Thess 2:8).

Pope Francis challenges us to avoid the temptation to think the work of evangelization and forming disciples takes place primarily in committee meetings, our offices, or even at the events and programs we offer. We should be so immersed in people's lives that we "take on the smell of the sheep" (Pope Francis, *Evangelii Gaudium*, art. 24). Investing time with people outside of the Wednesday night Bible study or Thursday morning mom's group may be just as important as the faith formation activities themselves—and our personal investment in their lives will help those activities themselves bear more fruit. Like Paul, let's give disciples not only the Gospel but our "very selves."

In short then, the word "disciple" simply:

- Is a person that wants to and is trying to become closer to God, AND
- Has a person in their life that helps them and models what that life can look like, AND
- Is a person who understands and commits that this knowledge and life with God will be passed on to someone who is not fully developed as a Christian but wants to be.

Any book on discipleship necessarily requires that we define in depth an understanding of the word and concept of a disciple—what it is and what it is not. In this section, I want to lead you through a mental process of understanding what a disciple really is!

1. How we got the term "disciple," historical usage, and
2. What Jesus meant when he used the term, and
3. Why/how I think the church has lost its real meaning.

Some feel that all believers are disciples, each at their own level. Some describe believers as each on their own layer with followers on the outside of a circle, and each is moving closer into the center which is Christ. Others believe the believer is on a rung, like a ladder, and each step they take is a rung closer to Christ.

I cannot argue with these concepts. I just believe two things:

1. A disciple has another person in their life who is discipling/mentoring/coaching them and has a person they can go to when they fall, and
2. A disciple has in his/her mind to pass this knowledge on.

Historical Use of the Word "Disciple"

This is probably the most radical part of my discovery. Not only was I discipled in 1970 using this method, but history shows the word "disciple" was in common use LONG before Christ used it as recorded in the Bible. The concept of having disciples was in use hundreds of years before Christ.

Do you see the greatness of Jesus's method of making His disciples?

Answer: Jesus's method which had historical underpinnings/usage, but maybe, more importantly worked in the 1970s AND works now!

Socrates, who was born about 470 BC, was a disciple of Anaxagoras. Socrates, the developer/originator of modern Western philosophy passed on his knowledge/life/method to his disciples, among which was Plato (who lived from 428–347 BC). Plato, in turn, passed on and continued this method to one of his disciples, Aristotle (who lived from 384–322 BC).

Even common modern sources, like Wikipedia, say:

> The meaning of the word "disciple" is not derived primarily from its root meaning or etymology but from its widespread usage in the ancient world. Disciples are found in the world outside of the Bible. For example among the ancient Greek philosophers, disciples learned by imitating the teacher's entire way of life and not just by remembering the spoken words of the teacher.

DISCIPLESHIP

The first-century philosopher Seneca the Younger (4 BC–AD 65) appeals to the "living voice and intimacy of common life" of the disciple–teacher relationship of many different philosophers:

Cleanthes (320–230 BC) could not have been the express image of Zeno of Citium (334–262 BC), if he had merely heard his lectures; he also shared in his life, saw into his hidden purposes, and watched him to see whether he lived according to his own rules. Plato, Aristotle, and the whole throng of sages who were destined to go each his different way, <u>derived more benefit from the character than from the words of Socrates</u>. (Emphasis added)

In the world of the Bible, *a disciple* **was a person who followed a teacher, or rabbi, or master, or philosopher. The disciple desired to learn not only the word teaching of the rabbi, but to imitate the practical details of their life. A disciple did not merely attend lectures or read books, they were required to interact with and imitate a real living person. A disciple would literally follow someone in hopes of eventually becoming what they are.**

A Christian disciple is a believer who follows Christ and then offers his own imitation of Christ as model for others to follow (1 Corinthians 11:1). A disciple is first a believer who has exercised faith (Acts 2:38). This means they have experienced conversion and put Jesus at the center of their life and participated in rites of Christian imitation. A fully developed disciple is also a leader of others who attempts to pass on this faith to his followers, with the goal of repeating this process. (1 Corinthians 4:16–17; 2 Timothy

2:2). A special form of passing on leadership through discipleship is called apostolic succession.

Another Source for the Definition of "Disciple"

According to another source, "The Radical Discipleship Network" article by the Rev. Dr. John Hirt, A. M.:

> The word "Disciple" in Greek "Mathetes" is derived from the verb "to learn." Further, (the word Disciple) "carries the basic sense of being dependent on and of following a master of instruction." According to Rev. Dr. Hirt, this is not a one-time conversion or turning to God but rather, "Radical Discipleship" expresses the need for a perpetual re-orientation towards the essential teachings of Jesus." Rev. Dr. Hirt goes on, "Radical Discipleship is critical to the Christian life because it provides a genuine alternative to wooden fundamentalism and flaky liberalism. As such it stands over against a form of Christianity that has shifted from the core teachings and practices of Jesus and His kingdom."
>
> Another source puts it somewhat differently: "The Greek term "Mathetes" refers generally to any 'student,' 'pupil,' 'apprentice,' or 'adherent.' In the ancient world, however, it is most often associated with people who were devoted followers of a great religious leader or teacher of philosophy… In Isaiah 8:16 it says, "Tie up the scroll as legal evidence, seal the official record of God's instructions and give it to my '_followers_' "The Hebrew term for 'followers' is from the word which means 'to learn' or 'instruct.' Which may indicate that Isaiah had built up 'a circle' of Disciples whom he personally instructed and who

could promulgate his teachings among many in the nation. That is, while he may not have had a formal school, he, nonetheless, gathered around himself certain men and passed his teachings on to them. Note that Isaiah was alive and ministering from about 740 to 680 BC.

(In the RSV translation, I noted that the word 'followers' is replaced by "Disciples.")

Isaiah 50:4 (RSV) the writer says that, _"God wakes him every morning and gives him attentiveness so that he can listen and learn."_ In this way he is like a Disciple. Therefore, involved in the concept of being a Disciple is a willing, listening, and obedient heart.

In the Greek culture, the Greeks used the term to refer to a "learner" or on a more committed level, an 'adherent.'"

In summary, "There is (much!) evidence that personal discipleship was commonly used among the Greeks and the Jews. Though the term 'Disciple' is used in different ways in the literature of the period, there are examples of Discipleship referring to people committed to following a great leader, emulating his life, and passing on his teachings. In these cases, Discipleship meant much more than just the transfer of information. Again, it referred to imitating the teacher's life, inculcating his values, and reproducing his teachings." (Emphasis added.) (Source: Bible.org. From the series: _"Go and Make Disciples of All Nations."_)

"Disciple" As Jesus Used It

This concept of imitating Christ in being a disciple was not confined to the common usage of the word "disciple" but is confirmed in the Bible in 1 Corinthians 4:16–17 when Paul says, "For I become

DISCIPLESHIP

your Father in Christ Jesus through the gospel. I urge you, then, <u>be imitators of me</u>." Paul reiterates this concept in 1 Corinthians 11:1 (RSV) when Paul writing to the Christians in Corinth said, "<u>Be imitators of me, as I am of Christ.</u>" This verse also (importantly) emphasizes the concept and need for true discipleship, that of all leaders and disciples be imitators of Christ. Thus, in the end, disciple makers are guides to be watched and imitated as they are imitators of Christ.

Thus, it was well understood in Jesus's time what a disciple was and what it meant. It had more to do with following around and observing the behavior of the teacher/master. This was more than just words; being a disciple was (and should be today!) learning from the example of the teacher and an overt imitation of the teacher in the disciple's life.

This all comes from Jesus saying in Matthew 10:25 (RSV), "It is enough for the disciple to be **like** his teacher." And amplified instruction is given by Jesus in Luke's account: Luke 6:40 (RSV "A disciple is not above his teacher, but every one when he is fully taught will be **like** his teacher."

In Luke's account, in context, Jesus is absolutely talking about being a disciple in that Jesus says in the preceding verse, Luke 6:39 (RSV), "Can a blind man lead a blind man? Will they not both fall into a pit?"

Jesus is saying, we all need a teacher, a man that knows the truth and knows and "sees" the way, the route, a man should follow. This concept is so important! We ALL need a teacher, a discipler, to learn from AND model! We can and will never get to a point where we have got it all together as BMOC (Big Men of Christ). Wherever we are in this growth toward likeness path, we will always need this relationship in our lives!

So how does this happen? How do we find a man to follow that knows and sees the right ways to have this relationship with God? Mark gives an account of this (and other Apostles as well!) in Mark 1:17 (RSV) where he records Jesus as saying, "And Jesus said to them, <u>Follow me and I will make you become fishers of men.</u>"

So in considering who a disciple is, there is this element of a calling by God (through the Holy Spirit) to become disciples of His, to become followers of His.

Jesus Talks About What It Is To Be A Disciple

To get a handle on this, from Jesus's perspective, we need to start at the end and sort of back into a definition of "disciple."

Matthew 22:36 (RSV) says, "Teacher, which is the great commandment in the law? And He said to them, '**<u>You shall love the Lord your God</u>** *with all your heart, and with all your soul, and with all your mind. And a second is like it.* **<u>You shall love your neighbor as yourself</u>**. *On these two commandments depend (hang) all the law* and the prophets.'"

To boil that down, Jesus is saying you should follow / practice just two commands: 1) love God and 2) love your neighbor.

Then you get to Jesus saying as His last marching orders, his last command, the Great Commission when he said in Matthew 28:19–20, "Therefore go and make disciples…teaching them to observe <u>all that I have **commanded** you</u>" (RSV).

Do you see the progression?

- Jesus gave us God's two only commandments: love God with everything you've got and love one another, and
- Make disciples and teach them to observe all that I have actually COMMANDED you.

The marching orders to make disciples hang together with Jesus's two simple commandments.

If we, the church and every single person in it, really want to fulfill the Great Commission, we are to BE discipled and MAKE disciples.

All this taken into mind, when fully taught, a disciple will not be ABOVE his teacher, but will be LIKE his teacher (Ref: Matt 10:24).

Do you see the depth in this?

Being a disciple and discipling is more than a course simply taught, it is learning AND imitating the discipler AS HE IMITATES CHRIST.

(More on this imitation/emulate concept later.)

DISCIPLESHIP

Are All of Us Called to Be Disciples

Frequently I get asked, "Aren't we all called to be disciples as Christians?"

As you read this, consider your own leanings on this question.

The answers are important.

A calling, in my book, is a special appointment God has given you, a mission to be accomplished or attempted. Callings are special and reserved and come from God, not man. I don't think any human can come to you and say, "I think you have a calling to do this or that." I think humans/teachers, pastors, mentors, disciplers can <u>affirm</u> what God has already put on your heart.

I should insert here that when I say that God has put it on your heart, I mean God has somehow convinced you down deep in your soul that this thing that you are considering is an imperative, i.e., it is nonnegotiable—you just gotta do it!

So I would be careful in the use of the word "calling."

All are summoned/asked/hoped to become disciples.

Okay, then are we supposed to be disciples, and what's the difference between being a follower and being a disciple? This book attempts to answer that very question.

Is being a disciple some kind of special subcategory of Christians, like an inner circle, super Christian, or a special club or advanced Christianity? No.

I do not think this comes close to what being a disciple means. Rather, a disciple means someone who is intentionally seeking to know and grow closer to God AND someone who is intentionally being mentored/coached by someone to help them on this journey.

Then, what is to be if a person doesn't want to be discipled or to disciple others? Are they not in the will of God? And how does this relate to serving God by using our individual gifts? (1 Cor 12:1–31; Rom 12:6; and Rom 11:29).

And remember, we are all members of one body and should work together in unison.

Since this is a book on discipling and passing on what we have learned, it begs me to insert a word of caution.

DISCIPLESHIP

Before embarking on or into this discipling process, count the costs.

> For which of you, desiring to build a tower, does not first sit down and count the cost, whether he has enough to complete it. Otherwise, when he has laid a foundation, and is not able to finish, all who see it will begin to mock. (Luke 14:28)

I include this, only to say your new life with Christ may be radically different than you are currently living.

Jesus also talked about what it means to be a disciple, and we will get into each of the how to's, but consider just Jesus's two commands; think on Jesus's two commands and fulfill those, and you'll be a disciple of Jesus Christ.

Lastly, I would add:

If no one comes to you and wants to help you / train you and expresses as much, you should pray about it and may have to be assertive about it and go talk to another man and just say something like, "I see qualities in your spiritual life I would like to learn from and emulate. Can we set a time to discuss this further, maybe over coffee or lunch?"

I still firmly believe that we ALL need to be disciples and finding a more mature Christian to help or train you in walking closer with God!

Do We Really Make Disciples?

As shown in the preceding pages, the word "disciple" was probably in practice long before Christ came to this earth. Accordingly, it was a commonly known and used concept to have one discipler whom the others would follow, listen to intently, and whom the disciples would model.

It is this form of discipling that I believe this world and this current world's churches has watered down to the point of being not correctly known and, further, not practiced widely (!). The church today has adopted a group think philosophy where building larger and larger churches (including impressive edifices!) is the goal, not in-depth discipling through one-on-one relationships where deep growth and change can occur.

Small groups are good, but small groups do not develop the deep growth UNLESS an intentional purpose IN that group is for the leader to call out one (or two) guys in that group and start a one-on-one relationship, where more than just help, but that training is the aim. Guys in a small group must be intentionally taught to pray for, look for, and seek out a man to pour their life into AND to seek out someone to disciple, mentor, coach them.

Lastly, some have taken this concept WAY off the tracks. Some have used it to develop cults where the leader is the key, not Christ. Then others have even used it to enrich themselves financially (believe it or not!).

Why do I feel so strongly about this? It may seem like just a matter of semantics, but it is not.

The reason is how I was discipled and how those relationships have changed my life.

DISCIPLESHIP

When I was first discipled, we did things together. No, I did not follow my discipler around. We simply couldn't. We were both in the US Air Force with our respective jobs to do in obedience to those commanded over us.

However, it worked.

We did things like early morning devotionals or as we called them quiet times. We went sailing where I learned important concepts like there can only be one captain (which I learned after beaching the boat on shore. LOL. My mentor/discipler very calmly and quietly taught me that concept after practically sinking his boat and having to drag that boat from the shore around to the dock.)

These principles and lessons have stuck with me now—for almost fifty years! THAT is discipling.

We spent time in prayer, in Bible study, in witnessing, in memorizing scripture, and as mentioned above, in quiet times, but we did more; we travelled to conferences together like one in Rocky Mount, North Carolina, as we were both interested in it and getting together with like-minded men. I carried this method forward to my disciples, not out of obligation, but as events occurred and developed that we were both interested in like The Role of the Man conference, as we both wanted to be better husbands to our wives. Also, with another disciple, we went to a conference on Point Man, given by the author of the book by the same title, Steve Farrar. As we were both vets, we understood the concept of what it meant to be a Point Man in military exercises and excursions into enemy territory; knowing we were to lead our family through enemy territory, we wanted to know how to do it better. These are but just a few examples.

Gee? This Jesus method actually does still work in this current day!

THAT is why I wrote this book and why I encourage it, so it leads to a life of joy and of harmony. It has worked for me!

Where we get into trouble is when our own self-desires, self-wants rule. We feel the need to be right or win in an argument or do it our way.

God's way leads to harmony with God and with others.

This type of discipling simply works. I am proof of it and have seen proof of it in my own life and in my disciples as they carried it on to further generations (Discipling generations as well as offspring generations!).

A word of caution here, as I was recently very gently reminded by a kind, humble pastor and former discipler who, when I wasn't personally seeing fruit from my discipling, he reminded me, "God does the counting!" We "sow the seeds and God brings the growth" (1 Cor 3:6). So just don't worry about the growth; just adhere to Jesus's two commands and this way/method of discipling, and it will all work out for good!

I encourage you to consider this new (but old!) concept of the word "disciple"—that of being in a relationship with one other guy as we/you both just seek to imitate Christ.

Jesus had his guys follow Him around, taught them to pray, etc. We can now carry on that legacy now and build ourselves INTO a man's life as we imitate Christ.

I do fully recognize that we cannot follow someone around all the time and be with them all the time. We all have jobs and families. As an example of how it can work in today's life: one of my disciples and I met every week at a Denny's. The point here is: it can work, today!

My experience teaches me, there needs to be this on-on-one relationship with a discipler for real growth to develop. A church leader can talk about a believer taking the next right step. This is good and helpful in correction or change, but this limits the growth to what the person can/will do on their own initiative. I also think that leaders with this mindset miss Jesus's real meaning when He said, "Go and make disciples"; its common use at that time is missed. Jesus's message and method are clearly missed.

Is This Concept—And This Book— Just Meant for Men?

The answer is clearly and emphatically "No!" It is not just for men. The Bible's record of the early church is replete with examples of women disciples and even women leaders within the early church.

Also, my experience has shown me that this concept—one-on-one discipling—can have an invaluable effect on the women being discipled.

I have witnessed disciples of my wife go on to become disciplers and great leaders and encouragers within other churches across this whole country! What a loss if this were to be not utilized as the method to build one's self into another woman!!

Now I do believe firmly, a man, especially a married man, should NOT try to disciple a woman, unless the woman is the man's wife.

My reason?

The relationship involves some deep, deep intimacy that can cause real damage in a marriage if the man is discipling a woman who is NOT his wife!

Does This Place a Burden on Everyone Who Is Discipling Another?

The answer is "Yes!" unfortunately. My view on this is being discipled inherently must involve the understanding that this will be passed on. In my view, to just absorb and keep to oneself this invaluable training is just selfish; it is keeping this gift to yourself and not spreading it outward. (Also, keeping it just to yourself is not what God intended.)

So being a disciple DOES carry with it the burden that you will go on to disciple others.

The other "burden" (if you will) is that you need to seek to be able say to your disciple(s) as the Apostle did: **"Be imitators of me!"** Now this does not mean you have to be "perfect" to be a discipler, it (in my view) means you are just able to say, "Model my never-ending pursuit to grow closer to God in any way I can. Model my never-ending desire to simply obey His two commands: love God totally and with full abandonment, and love my neighbor."

A cautionary word should be inserted here and kept in mind as you read for further clarification of what a disciple really is! If you can

DISCIPLESHIP

ascend to the real use of the term "disciple" as someone who follows, observes, learns, and imitates the discipler, then,

1. One should be careful who they are being discipled by. This lesson should be held in full understanding of the tragic lives lost by the disciples of Jim Jones.
2. One must use common sense or the relationship can become one of dependence. The disciple, if not careful, can become dependent on a required presence by the discipler or from a point of view of needing approval from the discipler. The discipler's goal needs to be one of teaching the person to fish and not merely receiving fish or in this case: spiritual food. In other words, the disciple is eventually to have his/her own fully developed relationship with God, not <u>requiring</u> instruction from the discipler. However, once again, I must reiterate that even when full developed, a disciple needs to continue to BE discipled and in relationship with a teacher who the disciple can learn from and model.
3. In doing some historical research for this book, I discovered some of the ministries that have perverted the use of the words "disciple" and "discipling." There have been a number of discipling ministries that, even in my lifetime (!), have gotten WAY off-track.

The Shepherding Movement (sometimes called the Discipleship Movement) in the 1970s and early '80s was an influential and controversial movement. The doctrine of the movement emphasized the "one another" passages of the New Testament and the mentoring relationship described in 2 Timothy 2.

As Wikipedia mentions, "The shepherding movement arose out of a concern for the weak commitment, shallow community, and the general worldliness characteristic of many American churches. But their solution was extra-biblical requirements—membership in a house-group which included having life-decisions covered by the house-group leader, elder, or pastor. <u>Such decisions included things</u>

like where to live and work, whom to marry, or whether to see a doctor when someone was ill."

At the zenith of the movement, "They had a national network of followers who formed pyramids of sheep and shepherds. Down through the pyramid went the orders, it was alleged, while up the same pyramid went the tithes." The relationships that were formed became known theologically as covenant relationships. A network of cell groups were formed. Members had to be submitted to a shepherd, who in turn was submitted to the five or their subordinates. "Large numbers of charismatic pastors began to be shepherded by the CGM leaders, a development that went uncharted but not unnoticed. It was uncharted because these relationships were personal and not institutional, so there were never any published lists of pastors and congregations being shepherded by CGM leaders."

The Shepherding Movement became controversial. Figures within the charismatic movement (such as Pat Robertson) denounced the Shepherding Movement. Robertson used Christian Broadcasting Network (CBN) to pronounce the shepherding teaching as witchcraft and said, "The only difference between the Discipleship Group and Jonestown was the Kool-Aid."

What Can We Learn from Some Misguided Ministries?

- Is the focus on Jesus and His simple teaching?
- If a discipling relationship is established, is it Christ centered as opposed to Shepherd focused?
- Is it biblically based and underpinned?
- Simply put, watch out for decisions about your life that a discipler makes for you. This is so crucial! What your future holds and its direction is between you and your God!

DISCIPLESHIP

Three Things We Can Do to Make Godly Decisions

I was taught many (many) years ago there are several aspects to making Godly decisions in important matters:

1. What does the Bible say you should do?
   In any singular, less important decision, the instruction in the Bible is usually quite clear: don't do this / do this. In more grey areas, the Bible will still give overriding principles that will govern the decision, e.g., Does it bring glory to God? Does it contribute to the unity of the church? Is it loving?
2. Peace that passes all understanding.
   What the Bible says should/will match your inner peace on the matter. Speaking from experience, you WILL have this inner peace; you may not understand it or even be able to express it, but it will overwhelm you as the right, the peaceable thing to do.
3. Get Godly counsel. This means going to a Godly man and running it by him. (HINT: A listener not a lecturer)
4. Pray first with that person that God be there in that moment and in that discussion!)

What's the key here? Are these three in conflict with each other?
No! Just the opposite: All of these—if it is right in God's eyes—will line up together, be in sync with each other, and there WILL be harmony. Again, the peace Jesus spoke of will overwhelm you.

As said above, there are certain decisions that don't need to receive this kind of scrutiny. You know what to do and what not to do.

But on the important, life-changing stuff, these principles have never led me astray. Sometimes (okay, many times! LOL.) I have not been able to articulate why a decision has been made. I just know it in my gut and have confirmed it in scripture and with Godly men and gone forward with total conviction, I am on the right track.

DISCIPLESHIP

Summary on the Words "Disciple" and "Making" Disciples

These sections, especially on the historical basis for true discipling and Jesus's use of the word "disciple" should have taught you:

- The use of the term "disciple" originated around the time of Socrates and had an unmistakable meaning before Jesus used the term, and we have perverted its use, and
- When Jesus used the word "disciple," it was clear to those hearing it, and
- Discipleship was misused in the 1970s and '80s, and
- Over the years, the church has changed and watered down the true meaning of the word disciple/discipling.
- That the biblical discipling method has had an impact on me personally.

Why do I encourage it so much? It is because it leads to a life of joy and of harmony. Where we get in trouble is when our own self-desires and self-wants rule: We feel this NEED to be right or win an argument. THAT leads to disharmony. God's way leads to harmony.

Try it out!

My point here is not to defend the school and method of philosophy that Socrates taught. It is rather inserted merely to point out a couple of things:

1. Socrates gathered around him some students/learners, and they followed him around, listening, but even more, imitating his life.
2. Socrates originated a school where this was practiced; now, I believe, it is referred to as the school at Athens.
3. Socrates (470–399 BC) → Plato (425–347 BC) → Aristotle (384–322 BC)

The progression of knowledge and discipling demonstrates this passing on of his knowledge and, more importantly, his life to his disciples who in turn, passed on this method and teaching to their disciples and so on.

Is This a Practical Study of Discipling or Is This an Intellectual Study of Jesus's Methods

To be up front and honest with you, my original intent in writing a book on discipleship—Jesus's method—was to just explore how Jesus did it, i.e., chronologically, how did Jesus make disciples from the first meeting to the last instruction? Is there a chronological or by topic method to Jesus's method? However, recently, I have realized, we need to explore His last command first to fully understand the process or reason for Jesus's method.

This is not a scholarly work: a) I am not qualified to do that and b) many scholarly (and useful!) books have already been written on the chronology on Jesus's ministry like *Following the Master: A Biblical Theology of Discipleship* by Michael J. Wilkins, PhD, Fuller Theological Seminary and dean of the faculty at the Talbot School of Theology, Biola University, Zondervan Publishing, 1992.

A scholarly work was also never my intent. My intent has always been: a) to always follow God's leading on the subject, b) to make it orderly, i.e., follow some kind of logical structure, but more, to give the reader a glimpse of how other men have affected me and c) I think (and am hopeful/prayerful!) that God will touch some men with this book and turn up the flame a little (okay, a lot!) toward making disciples themselves!

Are we falling short or missing the target of His last command?

In this last year, I have realized the impact each man (and church) has added their piece to this whole thing in my life called being a Christian and, more specifically, discipling others.

As I sat here, completing the written work that started thirty years ago, I have come to the startling conclusion: Christ's way of discipling is actually very simple!

It is written down for us, with our simple minds, probably because he knew we could not comprehend it in all its mystery: We are so busy trying to remember to do all the things we think we are supposed to do, we forget what he told His disciples, His guys, many years ago.

This whole book is simply about ways to help others draw closer to Christ—that's it! You should be able to take any chapter, pull it out, and read it as simply another way you can draw closer to God.

We should, I think, have no other purpose in our discipling than a) to love God and b) to then help others along the way.

I read part of a book the other day (and plan to read it all once again to give it full measure) that a discipling could lead to a dependence of the disciple onto the discipler. It occurs to me: it could. If it's done in the wrong way, it could. But that's not necessarily true.

Discipling is not a series of things on a list or completing a course that needs to be checked off, and the disciple is then somehow qualified to disciple others. It is a relationship between one believer and another believer (probably a newer believer) where the discipler helps the guy along come closer to God, listening to and, thus, just loving the guy.

Discipling is not even just a book like this, that once completed, you've really got it! Some years ago, I went through a course by Greg Ogden, thirty chapters, which gave these basics and some good and on point reference materials, but immediately after finishing the book, I was left with the empty feeling in my gut, "What's next?"

Accordingly, I would urge you, after reading this book, to go through the Ogden thirty-chapter training wherein you learn and can teach:

- The basics of the Christian faith
- It will have you praying, reading, studying, memorizing scripture, not to fulfill a daily task list, but it is to learn a mental process where more and more of your unconscious and conscious focus is on God.
- <u>It should, however, be taken with the covenant to a) finish the course / finish the race and b) (importantly) to teach others.</u>

This teaching others is so important, it cannot be emphasized enough. It's not in Jesus's last command to become (good) disciples, rather it is to (go on and) make disciples, "teaching them to observe all that I have commanded you."

This book is probably going to offend many, and at some point, I may be accused of going into the temple and turning over the tables. If so, so be it, but we should not lose focus on growing the church to show that we are more right than others. There may be other methods to help guys (and girls) get closer to God, but if they become the end or if they take you away from just drawing closer, then, I am sorry to say, they've missed the mark.

Examples of Discipling Programs in Today's Churches

I have been to churches which were nothing more than an excuse to put together a praise band.

I have been to churches whose sole purpose was to build a building, a grand structure. Some erect big signs that say, "New Church Coming Soon!" One that my wife and I checked out when we moved from California was a church, inside whose walls were covered with plans for the new building.

We should be about building bridges to other Christians and to nonbelievers.

I have been to a church where the whole focus was on small groups, and somehow, out of these small groups would come ready to drive disciples! Woo-hoo! In these kinds of churches, you HAVE TO BE an extrovert and go out of your way to sign up for a group to meet anyone!

Most usually, the Leader will ask you to get up out of your seats and say, "Hello" (with a smiling face, even though at that very moment, you are broken or troubled). You might even catch their name, "Hi, I am Joe," but that's it—no real connection! Here's an idea, instead of preaching on a topic for twenty minutes, preach for fifteen, and ALLOW five minutes to really connect/find out something about them, like why they go there. Even more radical, a chance to meet someone and go have coffee or lunch with them!

DISCIPLESHIP

I am not saying Small Groups are bad, BUT I am saying discipleship does not come IN the group, rather, it is one guy developing a relationship with another guy FROM the small group with a similar or kindred heart and then you both walk through life together, meeting with each other. It can happen or begin in a number of ways. I set no limits on how God will act!

I have been to churches where one can go there on Sundays, and no one will even just come and say, "Hi! I am Joe, what's your name?" In almost all of these churches, you can come every Sunday (LITERALLY FOR YEARS) and stand at the back or in the lobby and no one will greet you or want to get to know you. You can go, hear some great praise music, which attunes you to praising God, not talk to a soul, hear the message, and go and leave without talking to anyone. No one, when you are leaving, asks you, "So what is your takeaway from what the pastor talked about?" Here's an idea. Instead of propping up some people with smiley faces to be greeters, ask people who feel this is their calling to really engage people, not usher them as going into a restaurant, to be watchful, and get to know who regularly comes to that service; remember their names (!) and make them really start to feel like family!

Church emphasis/practices and even methods or models they use do not upset me. I just observe, as in: I am watchful. God leads how He wants, and His will will be done and accomplished, and I am very comfortable with that. It is hurtful though to see how churches make it so easy for people to fall through the cracks, never meeting and getting to know a single other person. **One church I went to for years, and I never talked to or got to know one other guy.**

Put another way: how can a church say it is, "Love your neighbor as yourself," when that church cannot even love one another—as in the brethren, people believing much the same as you do?

I think the closest to observing (practicing) this part of the model was a vineyard church in the Bay Area of California. There, a guy met me when we came to worship with me and talking to me and getting my phone number for a way to get in touch with me, and I distinctly recall he called me a number of times, one to invite me to some activity: golf, football, or basketball probably (LOL). He stayed in touch with me. He was the assertive but welcoming one, trying to live out "Love one another."

For some time now, I have verbally referred to those having an impact on my life as reflecting a part of Christ. No one man has (or can) reflect all of the light, but I have seen parts of Christ in each of the various men who have impacted my life.

To explain that (and this will surely date me!), some of you may recall mirror disco balls, which were globe balls or globes that hung in the middle of the dance floor. Each disco ball was covered with hundreds, maybe thousands, of tiny pieces of glass or silver that reflect just parts of the spotlight down on the dancers as the ball turned around and around. Spotlights would be aimed at the disco balls, and each piece would reflect its small part of the light onto us as the globe turned around.

My view is that, since I became Christ's believer and follower, various men have come into my life and guided me and, in their particular way, have each reflected a piece of the light.

Paul, in his first letter to the followers in Corinth put it better: *"For now we see in a mirror dimly, but then face to face" (1 Cor 13:12 RSV).*

In reviewing that verse once again, I simply cannot wait to that moment to see Christ in all of His fullness, in all of His love for me.

You will see, as I explore how Jesus did it, how Jesus discipled His guys and, along the way, see how ordinary but real men have taught me, or I have observed, their particular reflection of Jesus.

My aim was originally to go through in one book from Jesus calling His first disciples (Luke 5:1–14) to the end where He called us all to *"Go therefore and make disciples of all nations…teaching them to observe all I have commanded you" (Matt 28:19, 20 RSV).*

My original intent was to just explore how Jesus did it, i.e., chronologically, how did Jesus make disciples—from the first meeting to the last instruction? However, recently I have realized, we need to explore His last command first to fully understand the process or reason for Jesus's method.

DISCIPLESHIP

Pay It Forward

These days, you may hear the expression "Pay it forward" often, like when you are at a toll booth on an interstate highway and someone in the car in front of you pays your toll for you. That is paying it forward.

My life as a Christian has had that done for me; the ones I have met along that walk have each given me pieces—their particular piece—of the picture. No one man has had it all together. Many though have humbly (and often joyfully!) passed it on to me, usually in the hope that I will in turn pass it on to others.

In Paul's second letter to his spiritual son, Timothy, Paul said this, "**_And what you have heard from me before many witnesses, entrust to faithful men, who will be able to teach others also_**" (2 Tim 2:2 RSV).

This next point, in connection with being a disciple and of making disciples and, although borrowed from some speaker or teacher in my past, is so particularly important:

Each of us need to have three people in our lives:

- One teacher:
    - This is that one person we can go to, not out of dependence but maybe out of respect, which is either helping or training us to be Christ's disciples and make disciples.
- One person who is not enamored by us!
    - This person can be brutally honest with you but does it with brotherly love.
- One disciple: one man we can pour our lives into and where we can invest our lives.
    - There's a lot to this last one. We will get to that.

Although I am not confident at this writing of its various form or forms, one thing I know it was never intended to be was an unabridged encyclopedia of all texts and information on the subject of the discipleship. In my heart, it has always been intended to be practical, not merely intellectual. It was and is only meant to lay out my experience and struggles as an example of what God does in a man's life and how it can work in your life and the men He gives you to minister to. Finally, I am not qualified to give an intellectually complete discourse on the subject nor do I feel compelled to include all of the references available on the subject. I only am compelled to bring forth how the person of Christ has affected me in this process of becoming His disciple and tell of the training and help others have provided me along the way in hopes that the process will be understood and that it will be continued in its right and proper perspective and form.

I would hope this would be intensely practical, motivating to action and not just thought. I would hope that from this, you would be challenged to seek God more, experience Him more fully, and as a result of that, be ignited to help others enjoy this same process—this sometimes painful, but always exciting process of change, a change from changing from un-holy to Holy, being ever and always changed more into the likeness of Christ. I would hope the Spirit would take aspects or chapters and challenge you to go deeper into that relationship to seek Him more in prayer, to seek Him more through His Word.

God originally designed us to walk in His Way. I believe there is a way to walk with the Lord and still be in this world. It is my hope that you find some of that experience in this book/manual, and that in it, God touches you where you are at and that God then begins to walk with you in that particular aspect of your life and that as a result you are changed and come just a little closer to (as the Bible says) "abiding in Him" (John 15:7).

Accordingly, as this book is meant to be practical to help you in your walk (the daily living out of your ordinary life while still keeping a good and open relationship at all times with your heavenly Father), this book is divided into chapters:

- Explaining what it is to be a disciple
- Making disciples without it merely becoming method

It takes the topics of a disciple's life of simply growing closer to God and explores each and lastly,
- Examining the process of discipling and in concrete, doable steps, outlines how you can lead another in his walk.

Thus, this manual can be used:

- By individuals seeking:
  a) to become better disciples and/or
  b) for some to inquire into how they can BE discipled or seek out others TO disciple.
  In plain English, this book is for guys who WANT to be more like Christ. Most pastors would agree that finding that one hour on Sunday or even small group studies aren't working or it isn't working trying to do it on your own.
- By men or women in a men's or women's ministry setting, either one on one (preferably) or in a group discussion, with follow-on ministry to go on one-to-one.
- By men with their wives in an exciting exploratory way that will lead to simply unbelievable depths of intimacy between the two of you!
- By pastors as they reexamine what true discipleship means—as Jesus taught and Jesus lived and not what the church has devolved into. In plain English, this book is also for pastors who have not experienced being discipled or have lost or are not experiencing the fruit from discipleship.

This is not written because I have gotten it right and have perfected it. It is simply that this method has had a profound impact on me and others and that I feel or am led to say that this has gotten virtually lost in the church today. Even further, my telling of this method, this life change, by ME, is more proof that it IS of God. It proves beyond any doubt I am human, and He is God! LOL.

One would think that you, the reader, would like to hear from some great leader or some great and well-known pastor. Well, I am neither. I am just a guy who has been touched by God's forgiveness and touched by some of His disciples who came alongside me and helped me stay on the path (or get back on the path when I fell off!) Now answer to yourselves, very personally, just you and God, would you like to be mentored or coached by God?

I have been an elder in a church, leader of several men's ministry groups, and over a number of years, have discipled a number of guys, but that's not to my credit as <u>God</u> brought the growth.

Writing this book is because a) this slow, gentle discipleship process has influenced me, b) I don't think a lot of guys know about it or are experiencing it, and c) I don't think but maybe 1 in 10,000 churches really get it, apply it, or emphasize it as the core of building believers.

Also, I have this deep-seated knowledge that I am to do my part: if it is God's message (not mine), then He will get it to those He wants to have hear it. I don't need to worry about that or the success of the book; I am just to do my part in this continuing process.

For the skeptic pastors (who are still reading!) and those of you who have been Christians for a while, let me ask you a few hard questions:

- Who are you building your life into—two to three men or the whole congregation, i.e., the once-a-week followers?
- Are you building your life into your leaders or working to make sure correct biblical teaching is modeled, taught, and passed on?
- Does this flow to every member of your church or does your church have this as their true core belief? Is this the key thing you teach to all believers, to get connected and be a disciple, then Disciple others?
- Do you really believe Jesus's command in Matt 28:19–20 was an imperative command or just an advisory, like "It would be a good idea"?
- Do you believe discipleship is a course or program or the very core of building Christian lives?
- Does the concept resonate in your soul, or is it a nice idea?

- Are you driven (like me) to continue in Jesus's footsteps and is this something God has put on your heart as "Yeah, that is just what I have been thinking"?

If so, read on!
And enjoy!
I genuinely believe John 10:10 when Jesus said, ***"I came that that they may have life, and have it abundantly"*** (RSV). I believe Jesus came to not only lay down His life for us that we might re-establish a right relationship with God, but also, to show us a way to live life in this world, a way of life that works.

The church has led us to believe that we can go to church once a week, for an hour, and that is going to bring us the abundant life and many are left wondering why they are not experiencing the abundant life.

What does this abundant life look like? Can we really "walk in the garden with God in the cool of the day" as once did?

We get mired down in a lot of rules or gotta-do's—like I have to be all those good things and have "love, joy, peace, patience, kindness, goodness, faithfulness, gentleness, self-control" (Gal 5:22 fruit of the Spirit) all the time! No wonder so many are not happy! They feel guilty because they missed one or two (or more) of the above.

(Hint: If you EVER get to that point where anything related to the relationship with God is a gotta-do, then stop in your tracks, take a step back, walk out that door, and just walk and talk with God for a while.)

Let's face it: we can't be perfect; we are predisposed to mess up.

So instead of trying to BE perfect, try focusing on the two imperatives and stop fighting our own tendencies. I think if we don't fight what God nudges us to be or do and we just love Him and (try to) love others, we will find a LOT (!) of joy, peace, patience, etc., etc.

So how do you get there?

Well, after banging my head against the wall for many years, I think the key is simply 1) realize that God's way works, and then 2) just listen.

DISCIPLESHIP

Making Disciples Is Not Meant for Everyone

These words are not meant for the unbeliever to convince them OF God's love or of His power to act and change for good. God does that work; we merely plant the seeds, the introduction to Christ, AND water the plantings (disciples)!

There is a verse that speaks to this:

John 8:47 says, *"He who is of God hears (and understands) the words of God; <u>the reason why you do not hear them is that you are not of God.</u>"*

There are other verses that speak to the fact that the things of God are only revealed to those who know Him; spiritual things cannot be understood by nonbelievers. Paul put it this way in 1 Corinthians 2:6–7, 14, *"Yet among the mature we do impart wisdom, although it is not a wisdom of this age or of the rulers of this age, who are doomed to pass away. But <u>we impart a secret and hidden wisdom of God</u>, which God decreed before the ages for our glorification… <u>The unspiritual (natural) man does not receive the gifts of the Spirit of God, for they are folly to him, and he is not able to understand them because they are spiritually discerned.</u>"*

And when we then tend to get haughty and think we are BMOCs (Big Men of Christ), that we have it all spiritually together, and we think we are indeed great teachers, remember what Paul said about His own ministry in 1 Corinthians 3:5–9, *"What is Paul? (Answer) Servants through whom you believed, as the Lord assigned to each. I planted, Apollos watered, <u>but God gave the growth.</u> He who plants and he who waters are equal… For we are fellow workers for God; you are God's field, God's building."*

Now that we all understand that we are all of the same level—that no one is greater than the next—let's proceed.

Encouragement

Jesus said, *"Come to me, all who labor and are heavy laden, and I will give you rest.* **Take my yoke upon you, and learn from me**; *for*

I am gentle and lowly of heart, and you will find rest for your souls. **For my yoke is easy, and my burden is light**" (Matt 11:29–30 RSV).

Even today, those words are reassuring, encouraging, and an unloading of any burden I think I might have, like when I took the eighty-pound pack off my back as I climbed Mount Whitney. I felt lighter than air. I was ecstatic! Are you carrying around a burden of gotta-do's, thinking you just have to do these things to be a disciple of Christ in order to not feel guilty? (You can actually be an ordained pastor and be asking this question, "Why do I feel so burdened down?")

Start taking a walk with God in the garden. No pack, no burden—unload it. It's just a walk in the park!

Start it today!

The entire (!) rest of this book is to encourage you to walk with Him. That's all it is. That's all discipleship is about: learning once again or maybe for the first time: **God wants more than anything just to walk with you.**

Origins of the Walk with God

God made man and woman and put them in the Garden of Eden to till it (i.e., for man to keep it up).

God apparently used to also walk in the Garden.

God came to them *"walking in the garden in the cool of the day"* (Gen 3:8 RSV).

Although man was put there to take care of the garden, I don't see where, <u>at that point</u>, the care of the Garden was hard work or pain. The hard work and pain came later <u>after they had sinned, not doing what God specifically told them</u>.

It had to be pleasant during at least parts of the day. God came to them (woman had then been created) *"<u>in the cool of the day.</u>"* Is your walk with God a pleasant walk in the park "in the cool of the day?"

Now, both men AND women, close your eyes and think of walking in a lush, tropical garden, full of life and green trees bearing a lot of fruit, and yet it's cool, not hot, with maybe a slight breeze with your best buddy.

This is what God wanted then and wants now.
This is how good and pleasant it can be!
God always meant life to be just a walk in the garden.

With a correct understanding of the Bible, our entire Christian life can be summed up in and built around a couple of simple, memorable statements/commands that Jesus gave us:

- Jesus only gave us two commands:
    o Love God with all your heart, all your soul, and all your mind, and,
    o Love your neighbor as yourself (from Matt 22:35–40).
- Jesus gave us simple marching orders:
    o Go make disciples (from Matt 28:19–20).

This book will challenge each of you (even pastors!) to examine your life in a totally new and refreshing and liberating way! It will require you to be open to new perspectives and to set aside some of your long-held beliefs of what the fully developed Christian looks like. It will break down and correct some commonly practiced methods and, in a new way, define anew what discipling (or in modern terms: mentoring or coaching) should look like.

This book will show you how to have an ever closer and closer relationship and walk with God. It will show you how you can have another person in your life you can turn to, to help you get there. "There" is to experience a close, moment-by-moment love relationship with Christ. It will not teach you a lot of things you must do, which I call gotta-do's!

The book is broken down into:

- Establishing and nurturing a love-relationship with God and,
- Redefining the word "disciple" and showing how it is lived out and
- You can be coached AND learn to coach others!

Interested?
Read on!
Consider:

- the Bible as your instruction manual.
- the church as a hospital where you go to get patched up, connected, and praise Him for His love for us.
- your disciple maker as your guide, meeting you where you are and helping you along the walk. (Hint. Hint. Your odds of meeting a guide are enhanced greatly if you go to an actual church or a small group within a church.)
- When you seek out and find and ask a discipler to help you, consider seriously helping someone else along the path of the walk. ***"And what you have heard from me (Paul talking) before many witnesses, entrust to faithful men, who will be able to teach others also"*** (2 Tim 2:2).

Jesus admonished us to consider the cost (Lk 14:28) and for us to "take up our cross and follow Him." Along the way, we need to consider both of these elements. It's not just a one-time commitment; it's a day-by-day consideration and relinquishment (of our life and in major and minor decisions), in our walk with God.

So let's go for a walk! Shall we?

Jesus's Commands Boil Down to Only Two Commands

Love God

When you allow God to come into your heart, you are excited to your core, and in your mind, you just know, although you cannot see it, it makes sense in your conscious and subconscious mind.

It's a loving relationship—Christ and you—whether it is the first time it happens, or years later, when you come back to Him and He welcomes you with open arms and is overjoyed to have that relationship renewed.

When you enter into this relationship, it is in love and only has a couple of requirements of you. Jesus said it clearly when he said, "*You shall love the Lord your God with all your heart, and with all your soul, and with all your mind*" (Luke 10:27 and Matt 22:37, referred to the Old Testament Deut 6:5). He also said, "*You shall love your neighbor as yourself,*" but we will get to living out that neighbor thing (in a moment).

This relationship is a loving relationship—much like when you fall in love with your sweetheart: You're not sure at first, but you know this is the one! When you are in love, you WANT TO spend time with her, you think about her. Loving God is the same thing—sort of.

God wants us to experience Him more and more, so in a sense, we go on dates with Him, in reading about Him, studying Him, having some quiet times, some call it devotionals, pray to Him, commit some of the neat things he has said to memory, etc.

When you are in love, you don't have a list of things you MUST DO every week with your sweetheart. You have things you WANT TO DO, like talk to her daily, sometimes many times daily. You don't HAVE TO go out on a date on Friday night with her—you WANT TO. You look forward to that date!

The short version of this lived out is if you are NOT having this type of loving relationship with God, START doing some things that bring you closer to Him (mentioned above). The more TIME you spend with Him, the closer you will come to Him. You will feel His gentle, loving nudge more often. You will see Him, understand Him more clearly, and frankly, sometimes, you will be simply drop-jawed amazed and in awe of Him.

Francis Chan put it this way in his book *Crazy Love*: "We never grow closer to God when we just live life; it takes deliberate pursuit and attentiveness."

1) What does the Word of God say "discipline" is?

When I think of discipline, I think of rules and regulations as to conduct, things to be practiced every single day. I think more about the relationship as one of love, not "I have to do this or that!" Maybe a better word for discipline is **habit**!

I have a habit of kissing my wife each night as we go to bed and as she walks out the door to go to work. I do it out of love. Yes, it is a habit, a good habit as I take that moment and express my love for her in one simple act. We do it, not because we must, we do it because it's a remembrance of the fact that, even if we argued the night before, we still love each other.

All disciplines can be those **habits** that bring you closer to God on a regular basis, not because you HAVE TO, but because you WANT TO.

DISCIPLESHIP

It is interesting that the Gospels do not talk of or mention the word **"discipline"** at all. Paul's letters to the churches do mention it.

> Fathers, do not provoke (NIV "exasperate") your children, instead, bring them up in the training and **discipline** (NIV "instruction") of the Lord. (Eph 6:04 RSV)
>
> And have you completely forgotten the word of encouragement (RSV "exhortation") that addresses you as a father addresses his son. It says, "My son, do not make light of the Lord's **discipline**, and do not lose heart when he rebukes you, because the Lord **disciplines** the one he loves, and he chastens (RSV "Chastises") everyone he accepts as his son." Endure hardship as **discipline;** God is treating you as his children. For what children are not **disciplined** by their father? If you are not **disciplined** and everyone undergoes **discipline** then you are not legitimate, not true sons and daughters at all. Moreover, we have all had fathers who **disciplined** us and respected them for it. How much more should we submit to the Father of spirits and live! They **disciplined** us for a little while as they thought best; but God **disciplines** us for our good in order that we may share in his holiness.
>
> No **discipline** seems pleasant at the time, but painful. Later on it produces a harvest of righteousness and peace for those who have been trained by it. Therefore, strengthen your feeble arms and weak knees. Make level paths for your feet, so that the lame may not be disabled, but rather healed. (Heb 12:11–13 NIV)

Note: In just this one passage, Luke uses the word "discipline" ten times.

Being one that does not like the routine, in contemplating the God-me relationship, I don't see this or read this instruction as setting out a set of to-do's or set of points you must earn to measure up or get into this exclusive club for disciples.

Rather I see it as being open enough or attentive to God's leading, correction, instruction.

2) Loving God vs. Obedience

As I was rereading C. S. Lewis book *Mere Christianity* recently, I read (but cannot find right now) his quote that "It is our primary responsibility to love God with all our heart, soul, and mind but that Loving God leads to obedience."

As we draw closer to God, He will ask us, if we listen while praying, difficult questions or give each of us difficult to hear instructions, Like "Go and be reconciled to your wife, admit that you were wrong." (BTW, if you go now/right then and follow His instructions with a cleansed heart, your love will usually be met with love from her side!)

So in these cases, our closeness to Him demands obedience to what he tells us, no matter how hard it is. We may put up a resistance, but I will tell you from experience, it's not healthy to try and arm wrestle with God!

He wins and you are uncomfortable.

Where I think a lot of Christians get stuck or side-tracked in their Christian lives is making the disciplines the aim. As C. S. Lewis would put it, <u>"God is interested in the character of the man, not his actions."</u> If any of the disciplines become a burden, then we have missed the point and should go back to square one, where we learn God loves us and just wants a relationship with us, to "walk in the cool of the garden in the afternoon."

These leadings from God, which bring us to obedience from His command(s), are not antithetical to Him at all, and we simply need to realize where He is coming from: He wants us to obey because of His love for us, much like a good Father would want for his kids. He simply does not want us to fall and get hurt.

DISCIPLESHIP

This reminds me of an example where God intervened in my thinking and my life. As I indicated, I married Sue in 1988 and with that came a beautiful but very headstrong girl named Kellie. Time after time, Kellie disobeyed some (rather meaningless!) rule or instruction, and I would put her on restriction, which meant something like no TV for one week. (Humorously, this often involved me in taping some computer paper over the screen to her TV! To this, I am told sometime later, she would just remove the paper!)

Then I would go back to my bedroom and sit (in anger) on the side of my bed! Then, and I can't remember exactly how it came into my brain or my heart, but I would hear this voice in my head saying, "Gary, you need to GO BACK and be reconciled to her AND JUST LOVE HER!"

So then, I would humbly go back and say something like, "Kellie. I am sorry, and you are not on restriction." (In all honesty, I didn't always respond and go and apologize! Kellie would affirm this! LOL)

God sees ahead and where disobedience might lead. In my earlier marriage example, He sees it might lead to a brick wall being built between my wife and I, and He doesn't want that. (I am convinced He wants marriages to work and be healthy and happy relationships and does not desire they break up. In fact, at times, you may look back and see how God has been the glue that kept the marriage together.)

When I talk about a brick wall, I am talking about all the bricks, which are like problems or issues not dealt with in a marriage that build up, and over time, you don't see it. They are just little issues—unresolved issues—that over time build a wall between you and your wife. The wall is there, and it is not good. So my wife and I purposed early on, intentionally, not to let the bricks build up.

There is biblical basis for correctly handling this process (as there are for almost every area and encounter in our lives!).

Ephesians 4:26 says, "Be angry but do not sin; do not let the sun go down on your anger, and give no opportunity to the devil." (In all honesty, I have not always heeded this clear biblical advice!)

That doesn't sound like a demand or even a requirement; it's just good advice, and you avoid adding a "brick" to that wall you have with whomever you are "mad" at!

Hmmm.

BTW, God wants this very close relationship with you—more than you do!

Amazing, huh?

That's right, God loves us and wants to be near us FAR MORE than we could even imagine.

THAT blows me away!

A question might arise when you hear the three elements in that verse: heart, soul, and mind.

Why THOSE three elements and what does each mean lived out?

(One can and should think on and try to apply this for, quite literally, the rest of our lives)

How can I love God with all my heart, all my soul, and all my mind?

That's pretty much all of me, isn't it?

Yep. Exactly!

It encompasses our total being, not just our conscious mind, not even the feelings in our heart.

Think on the three elements here: heart, soul, and mind.

- Why does loving God in our heart come first?
- What does each of these three parts of us mean?

Heart, I believe, is your emotions, your feelings, your heart throb (to continue the love relational feelings when you are in a loving relationship with another person.)

In this, I realize, as in a personal relationship, it can be up, very high, but sometimes, deep down, we are human.

It also means you can decide to take a break, have some space. You can even walk away from God and not have anything to do with Him for years! I know because I experienced that. For a period, after the military service, I walked away, not because I was angry at Him; time with God then was just inconvenient. It took time away from watching football games on Sundays; it ate into my day! Dumb I know, but it can happen.

The strange part of this is JUST like the prodigal son, God was waiting there, grinning from ear to ear, simply happy to talk with me again, spend time. He was ecstatic to see me again and welcome me back with open arms. If you, too, have stepped away for a while, please know this: that God wants you back. He is MADLY in love with you!

How Do We Actually Love One Another?

This is the tough one because it literally commands that we step out of our comfort zone and DO SOMETHING. The First Command is internal: love your God; that's personal between you and God. This one deals with interaction between us and brothers and sisters of the faith and/or people we do not even know.

The questions become:

- What does it really mean: "Love your neighbor…as yourself?"
- How do we truly practice what this says, what Jesus COMMANDED us to do?

The actual concept or "love your neighbor" and "love one another" predates Jesus (maybe even to the Middle Kingdom 2040–1650 BCE) and is a principle having to do with reciprocity, this idea that we should treat others as we would like to be treated.

Jesus said it, but even His words derive from the Old Testament Laws in the third Book of Moses called Leviticus. Leviticus 19:33–34 reads:

> *When a stranger sojourns with you in your land, You shall do him no wrong. The stranger who sojourns with you shall be to you as the native among you and* **you shall Love him as yourself,** *for you were strangers in the land of Egypt; I am the Lord your God.* (RSV)

Jesus said it, but further, Jesus COMMANDED it!

He didn't leave us hanging there. Jesus gave them an example, which they all would understand: the story of the GOOD Samaritan (Luke 10:25–37). Here, Jesus illustrates how we not only should go out of our way for strangers, but also, those who are despised by the elites, the do-gooders who won't stoop for such a lowly person, or (to use a vivid example) stop, get out of your car, and help someone in need.

Sometimes (more like occasionally) to my wife's horror and sometimes to my endangerment, I do this: I pick up strangers, obviously in need, and do what I can, get them food take them where they need to go. Sue and I have taken in homeless people, one from a church who had two sons, who we learned later was actually possessed, who, hearing that a prayer group we were part of in that church were coming to pray over our house, fled hurriedly, with all their belongings in a shopping cart, shouting more obscenities at me personally than I probably have ever heard, as I drove up to the house after work.

In detailing what he really meant, in the Sermon on the Mount, we are told not only love them, but to "turn the other cheek" and "love one's enemies."

Question

Is that kind of "love one another" carried out today? It seems like we are trying to beat our enemies into submission every day of contemporary life in politics and in people climbing the ladder to success!

To answer the question, "Are we to love just the brethren or everyone?" I think it was answered succinctly by an American Evangelical Theologian Francis Schaeffer when he suggested that "Christians are not to love their believing brothers (and sisters) to the exclusion of their non-believing fellowmen. That is ugly" (Schaeffer, Francis A. 2006. *The Mark of the Christian.* Inter-Varsity Press. ISBN 978-0-8308-3407-5).

Jesus answered the question first when Jesus was asked, "But who is my 'neighbor'?" and Jesus gave the example of the Good Samaritan (Luke 10:25–29).

DISCIPLESHIP

Jesus gives other examples to show the depth of this command. In John 15:12–13 (RSV), He said, *"This is my commandment, that you love one another as I have loved you. Greater love has no man than this, that a man lay down his life for his friends. You are my friends if you do what I command you."*

In many places, the church (all believers) is referred to as Christ's Bride.

By extension and application to us now, putting that concept of the Bride with the concept of laying His life down for the bride, dying (!) was the greatest and clearest example of just how much Jesus loved/loves us!

Think on that one a bit.

To further delineate what that means in real life as the husband's responsibility in Ephesians 5:25, we are told, *"Husbands, love your wives just as Christ loved the church and gave Himself for her"* (NIV).

Question: Are you really to give up all of you for your wife, your dreams, ambitions, your thoughts, your position in arguments? (Ouch!)

Further instructions for husbands follows in Ephesians 5:28, *"In this same way, husbands ought to love their wives as their own bodies. He who loves his wife loves himself."*

Finally, Jesus, in His last prayers to His Father, prays about (and thus "talks" about) how we are to treat other believers in John 17:1–26 described or labeled as Jesus's high priestly prayer. Jesus prays for all the believers that there be unity and that takes love (starting with vs. 20), *"I do not pray for these only, but also for those who believe in me through their word that they may all be one; even as thou Father art in me, and I in Thee, do that the world may believe that thou hast sent me."*

Maybe you have read those verses or thought about it a little, but please realize the gravity of those few words:

If there is not unity in and amongst the believers, they, who do not believe in Jesus, cannot believe that the Father sent Jesus! If there are disagreements, anger, or arguments among "the brethren," then the nonbelievers cannot believe! It takes love, sometimes extraordinary love, to have this unity in the church exist.

Jesus's Last Marching Orders (Matthew 28:19–20)

This section of the book is formatted a bit differently, but I think gives more practical guidance that we can do and be as well as what we can and should be teaching our disciples. It breaks down Jesus's last marching orders word by word, phrase by phrase into small segments that can be better understood and put into practice.

Matthew 28:19–20 (RSV) in total says, **"Go therefore and make disciples of all nations, baptizing them in the name of the Father and of the Son and of the Holy Spirit, teaching them to observe all that I have commanded you; and lo, I am with you always, to the close of the age."**

Let's now take each part of those instructions and examine them more closely. Remember, there is a danger in adding to or leaving out ANY part of God's Word!

"GO"

Jesus's word "Go" here was an imperative, not a suggestion. He did not say: "I have this Suggestion" OR "Go, but only if it's convenient for you. I don't want to impose" OR "Go, if you have time" OR "I want you to think about making disciples."

Now, we simply must Go!

So does that mean we <u>must</u> go Africa or Siberia or some other end of the civilized world? Not necessarily, but God may be calling you to commit to do just that right now.

But it still is an imperative for each one of us. So how do we react?

Inferred in His command to Go are the following two caveats:

1. You must BE a disciple before you can MAKE disciples, and
2. You are to Go and not just learn stuff and feel all good about how righteous you have become and keep it to yourself but the rather go and make disciples!

We Go as He instructed His guys, His disciples. First, we must be disciples, then spread His living and loving words in our own lives and words in order to teach others. This infers you know and have in your own life what you are about to teach! Sounds simple enough, you don't Go and teach a college level course on biometrics unless you have tried it out and wear it.

This book will go into great lengths to describe what it means to be first a disciple and then a disciple maker and further to become makers of disciple makers.

We Go as servants first as humble servants of our Lord and God and then as servants of those we teach. But, Gary, how do we do this?

Jesus had told His guys earlier in His teaching of them, *"And even as the Son of man came not to be served, but to serve, and to give His life as a ransom for many"* (Matt 20:28 RSV).

So we Go! humbly and as servants to others. We don't go as haughty know-it-alls, the ones that have it altogether. We Go to help and serve others.

Preceding that verse, Jesus had told them not to get self-righteous, *"But Jesus called them to Him and said, 'You know the rulers of the Gentiles lord it over them, and their great men exercise authority over them. It shall not be among you; but **whoever who would be great among you must be your servant, and whoever would be first among you must be your slave'"*** (Matt 20:25–27 RSV). Wow!

You've all probably heard the saying, "A leader leads"; well, he leads by being or becoming a servant of those he leads. I asked a great leader I served under while at the FBI, who later became an AD or assistant director, if he believed in and practiced servant leadership.

He replied almost instantaneous and happily, "Oh yes! I believe in that completely!" He understood what I was talking about.

Consider the following things Jesus did at the last supper—His last time with His guys—knowing the importance of every single thing He was saying and doing, knowing full well he was about to be crucified:

> *Jesus, knowing that the Father had given all things into His hands and that He had come FROM God and was going TO God…rose from supper, laid aside his garments and girded himself with a towel. Then He poured water into a basin, and began to wash His Disciples feet, and to wipe them with the towel with which He was girded.*
> (John 13:3–5 RSV, Emphasis added)

Jesus went onto explain the significance of the example given by the washing of the feet: *"He who has bathed does not need to wash, except for his feet, but he is clean all over; and you are clean"* (John 13:10–12).

Jesus was not merely talking about the outward bathing or cleansing example. Jesus was talking about the cleansing that only He can bring to you by His indwelling in you. Later, when He had finished, Jesus said (importantly) to them:

> *Do you know what I have done to you? You call me Teacher and Lord, and you are right, for so I am. If I then, your Lord and Teacher have washed your feet, you also ought to wash another's feet. For I have given you an example that you should do as I have done to you.*

This infers this transfer or passing on principle: Jesus washed His disciples AND THEN turned to His disciples and said you ought to wash another's feet, just as Jesus had washed theirs! He left us His example.
(John 13:12–15 RSV)

Is this clear on HOW we are to Go?

Jesus was giving each one of us a lesson and an example of how to be a leader, a disciple maker. So Go! but with a right sense of who you are—humbly and with a servant's heart—always remember who you are now: you were bought with a price. It cost Jesus His life.

Go! Excited!

Go humbly by following His guidance (and not your agenda) day by day, moment by moment.

But GET MOVING!

"THEREFORE"

Matthew 28:19–20 verses start off with "Go <u>therefore…</u>"

I was always taught when you see the word "Therefore," find out **what the "therefore" is there for!**

If you back it up one verse, you discover why Jesus says, "Therefore…"

Matthew 28:18 (RSV) says, "And Jesus came and said to them, 'All authority in heaven and on earth has been given to me.'"

Whoa!

That's a pretty dramatic statement!

Do we really believe that? Do we believe Christ has ALL the power and that there is power in simply uttering His name, Jesus Christ?

Authority?

All authority, everywhere!

To understand who is telling you, "Go and make disciples," you need to realize who really is doing the talking here. Did or does He have the authority to give us marching orders or not?

In Matthew 28:18, just prefacing the marching orders to go and make disciples, Jesus said the most amazing thing: "ALL authority in heaven AND on earth has been given to ME" (RSV, Emphasis added).

"In heaven and on earth"? That encompasses about everything, doesn't it. Think deeper though; think of the wide expanse of the universe and thus of heaven. It's huge!

Okay, think of just the earth, but the WHOLE earth; that's a pretty big place, and He has coverage/authority there as well!

This is probably one of the most powerful statements in the whole Bible. It gives context and cites the reference as to what He is about to tell his disciples and, thus, to us.

So How Do We Make Sense of All This?

Okay, so it is clear from historic use and my personal experience that a disciple is someone who learns by being with and around a discipler, a teacher. I also think that inherent in being a disciple is the knowledge or charge that this is to be passed on to other newer disciples.

A disciple is one who inculcates the teachings of the Bible and of the discipler into every facet of their life as they imitate the discipler, who in turn is given charge to imitate Christ.

In the end, we desire to be disciples of Christ. This is a never-ending process, and along the way, men will (hopefully) come into your life and guide you / help you come closer to God. Being a disciple of Christ infers that you will pass this on to other men.

Do I distinguish between followers and disciples?

In a word, yes!

I believe (contrary to most church's current teaching!) that followers of Christ are people who believe in all that is Christ—his life, his death, and his resurrection—but who are not in the relationship of being discipled and all that means. In other words, I don't think a believer can properly operate and fully grow independently without someone in their life who is helping them grow closer to God, who gives them instruction, lives it out (walks the walk), and guides them. There is this relationship aspect where the disciple learns more from the life of the discipler than that disciple learns just from Bible studies.

Most churches today, I would say, almost without exception, use the term "disciple" too casually, i.e., some church leaders say we are all about making more and better disciples. However, in practice, they miss the mark by not including or insisting that the disciple be in a relationship with a discipler. I firmly believe that this word was used before Christ in the ancient philosophers and then by Christ himself. As you will see repeated many (!) times in this book: we need to be in relationship with a person who can disciple (or model) the Christ and we need to be passing this knowledge, this life, to other disciples.

This is the pure, clean use of the term "disciple," not what the church has turned the word into meaning for their own purposes. The real use and purpose of Jesus calling us to make disciples has become lost in the mediocre attempt to be all the church was meant to be.

Where a lot of Christians get stuck or held up is making the disciplines the aim. As C. S. Lewis would put it, "God is interested in the character of the man, not his actions." If any of the disciplines become a burden, then we have missed the point and should go back to square one, where we learn God loves us and just wants a relationship with us—to "walk in the cool of the garden in the afternoon."

In its essence then, God wants us to first be disciples, be in close relationship with Him, and THEN go and make disciples, replicate what you have in your life. (You can't do the second without the first!) The disciplines themselves do not become the end—the desired end result—they become the MEANS to that end, a very close relationship often called a walk with God.

The disciplines—the means to that end—can consist of any number of things surrounding God's Word, God's "notes" to us including:

- Hearing the Word of God, and
- Reading the Word, and
- Studying the Word, and
- Memorizing the Word—spending time and being able to connect with quickly what He has told us in His Word, and
- Meditating on God's Word—said in different ways: quiet times, devotionals, or just pondering the Word.

So what is to become of those not in a true discipling relationship?

My wife, Sue, and I have discussed this at length, and followers and true believers not in this discipling relationship can and should operate and fully utilize the giftings (1 Cor 12) that each of us have been given, serving the church each in their way. Serving in the gifting you were given can provide such joy, such indescribable joy.

Operating out of a position of knowing and living your gifting can and should (!) produce joy and peace—indescribable joy!

An example:

One of our neighbors discovered he had a hole in his heart, and it needed to be fixed! However, he was a diligent worker trying to do some landscaping at his residence. Accordingly, he had had a local company come and drop off a big pile of soil.

I saw the pile of dirt and talked to the wife about his condition, and then, walking across the street to our house, I thought, *I can help them by moving the pile of soil from their driveway to the back yard where they had intended to use it!*

I mention this NOT to give me any crown of glory whatsoever, but to get to the joy I felt in doing this, in serving and helping my neighbors! It's been a while now, but I DISTINCTLY remember actually singing hymns and spirit-filled songs while I was working; it was pure joy!

To give you the other side of the picture of me:

At a smallish church, I was involved in Bible studies, leading men's ministry, being an elder (and the resulting meetings), writing and printing off copies of a newsletter to the congregation, and what we called kid's church, where the little ones would go to another room, and I'd have a lesson plan (which took prep time!). Well, after a while, I got tired, and as I confessed to the pastor's wife that I had actually almost gotten mad at the kids carrying on and talking. She was astonished and, being the gracious woman she was (and is!), she removed that burden from me.

See, I was not operating out of a position of joy, I was filling what I felt I HAD TO do. Serving can and should be such a joy.

DISCIPLESHIP

"Make Disciples"

Think about the words "make" (disciples). Can we really make disciples?

Hmmm.

I don't think there's a bit of chance involved in or you and I deciding who is and who is not to be discipled. God goes before us, and our only trouble is getting our brains aligned with His heart and coming alongside Him and doing what work He has already begun!

Deuteronomy 31:8 RSV says, *"It is the Lord who goes before you; He will be with you, He will not fail you or forsake you; do not fear or be dismayed."*

In case, you want to see where else God goes before us here is strong biblical basis for this thinking. There are at least twelve other verses confirming God is already going ahead of you including:

- Exodus 13:21
- Exodus 14:19
- Exodus 32:1
- Exodus 32:23
- Numbers 14:14
- Deuteronomy 1:30
- Deuteronomy 1:33
- 2 Samuel 5:24
- Psalm 77:20
- Psalm 136:16
- Isaiah 45:2
- Isaiah 52:12

BTW, don't overlook these twelve additional verses! Go and look them up, and remember, <u>if you get a little discouraged sometimes</u> at work or in your marriage or with your kids, just pull out this book, look each one up and read it!

DISCIPLESHIP

Take one for example:

> <u>*I will go before you and make the rough places smooth.* *I will **SHATTER** the doors of Bronze and **cut through** their Iron bars.*</u> (Is 45:2)

Is that encouraging or what? BTW, I like that word "shatter"! It doesn't mean we need to go up to the door and ask, "Pretty please! Can you let me in! Pretty please with cherries on top?" We can and should go in boldness and with confidence!

From this, our principal job (at most) is to help the man get out of his own way, so God can do His stuff!

Just as Jesus did routinely (by going to the Father), I think we need more practice at this, and then we need more doing, that is, we need to have our hearts so closely aligned with the Father that (after CONSIDERABLE prayer) we will be able to go out, with every confidence, and KNOW who the Father wants us to train up as disciple(s).

This is a hard one for some of us. Some feel that we are all called to be disciples. I don't think the in-depth discipling God has put in my life and on my brain and in my heart was meant that way, i.e., invite them all and see who comes! Jesus simply went to the Father (in prayer), found out who the Father is already at work in, then Jesus went to that person (those people) and told him/them simply, "Come follow me, I will make you fishers of men!" As many noted, Jesus was not told to invite the elite, the smarter, those in high positions. He invited rather unintelligent fishermen and an (IRS) tax collector! Oh my!

This was a divine appointment.

Have you ever come across a divine appointment? An event that you knew in your heart was brought together by God Himself? We just need to realize who is doing the talking, who is doing the leading. When we do this, the person is apt to say something like, "You know, I was going to give you a call about this. It's been on my mind a lot lately!"

Think about it once more. Was it mere coincidence that Jesus selected these twelve disciples? Did he invite the masses like, "Come all who want to be my disciples." Or was it a divine appointment already in the works?

This selection process is one of the more interesting parts of His ministry and one that is often overlooked or misapplied. We, on the other hand, rush out there attempting to disciple guys before:

1. We have aligned ourselves with God's heart, AND
2. We give this a proper amount of time in prayer.

Once we have done these two things, we will KNOW who God wants us to disciple, and then we need to go out and do it: MAKE disciples. (BTW, Jesus went up into the mountains and prayed about this ALL NIGHT!)

To the point of MAKE disciples, I believe once we have selected the guys, there is action to be done on our part. God didn't just give us fully spiritually formed men of God. We are given men, but they come in the form of clay (some more gritty than others LOL) and (prayerfully) we are to help them ALLOW God to do a good work in them and ALLOW God to form them into His design (not our vision of what they should look like).

Are you getting the part and importance prayer has in all this—this whole thing of discipling? I think prayer is not just a good place to start and then it's done and on we go implementing OUR plan. There are a number of times when Jesus withdrew from His disciples to be with the Father. You know, I secretly think it was to consult with the Father on just what to do with all these knuckleheads, who were just not bright enough to get it! They didn't get it actually until Jesus left the earth and came back! (I call them knuckleheads, but I am no better! I should have caught on MUCH quicker since I am so MUCH smarter and knowledgeable than this bunch of fishermen and IRS agents!)

Okay, Jesus's last speech to His guys was the most important speech in His life and ministry. I think we need to think on this long and hard through the reading of this book and on into the future. It is often called His marching orders.

Okay go a bit further with me using that analogy:

Imagine General Patton, the most influential and commanding general in military history, giving this address. (Okay. Stay with me; it's an analogy!)

Patton addresses His guys and says, "I am the SUPREME Commander. ALL Authority has been given to ME by the Allied commanders!"

Don't you think what follows might just be kind of important?

With this in mind, go and reread Matthew 28:18–20, KNOWING Jesus has been given ALL authority, not just here on earth but heaven as well!

Jesus left a short clear message: "Go make disciples!"

However, I believe what follows explains how His guys (and us!) are to do it:

- Baptize them (the conversion process: the old is dead, you have a new life; more on that later).
- Teach them. I go into great detail later on HOW that is done.
- Teach them to observe, practice, give attention to.
- All that I have "commanded" you. Recalling, Jesus only gave two commandments!
- Remember, I am with you always.

That's Patton's speech in a nutshell, and it would have been his strongest and most powerful of his marching orders.

Okay, now for implementation of Jesus's marching orders, battlefield strategy and tactics. Just how in the world are we to actually MAKE anything?

Do we make disciples? That's what the Bible says to do, right?

BUT then again, Jesus did not say, "Go and sit on a park bench beside a lake and I will BRING disciples to you." It occurs to me that "make" is an action verb, requiring (!) us to somehow intervene into a person's life and affect change. Somehow, we are to take something that is NOT a disciple and (with GOD's help!) turn it into something that IS a disciple.

DISCIPLESHIP

I am going to speak extensively about this teaching aspect—the how to's—to help the guy understand and inculcate into his life various aspects of how to grow closer to and more aligned with God.

I think we sow and water, but God brings the growth. Remember that as you toil to see growth in a man! To me, this frustration is a little like sitting in a dentist's chair while the dentist works on my messed-up teeth. Looking back, it's not fun to remember, but the illustration works.

(Oh, great, Gary, yet another analogy! LOL.)

If I fight the dentist, it's much, much harder for the dentist to do his best work! When I relax, close my eyes, and trust in his hands, the dentist can (and has done) MIRACLES!

So our job in trying to make disciples is to help each man into the dentist's chair, to help the man let go of issues, and to help the man gradually relax into God's caring hands!

To continue with this analogy, discipling—making disciples—is not as much OUR doing, as it is helping each man, with his particular set of circumstances, trust God. Trust in each man's timing and trust in every area of a man's life. Our job then in making disciples is to acquaint the man with the dentist, helping this guy get to know Him better, then he can trust the dentist more and more until he is totally relaxed and basically <u>fall asleep in the chair</u>.

Is that it? Is that all God wants to say through me about making disciples?

I think if we envision ourselves as doing ANYTHING that brings glory to US, we are OFF-base!

I think if we envision anything we work on or discuss with a guy as something that might bring the man more into a closer relationship with the Father, we are ON track.

To give you some short takeaways from all this:

- Helping the guy understand who God really is and who Jesus is and studying THAT is good in discipling because the guy understands the dentist better. So ANY intake of the Word by hearing, reading, studying, meditating on, or memorizing is good if used for that purpose.

- I think prayer is good, useful, and necessary; it is the two of them—your guy and God—talking to each other, getting to know each other better, and that is good.
- Verse memory is important in the making of a disciple as it helps your guy meditate on God and not the NBA Finals score or an attractive woman who passes by!

Thus, I think there are a great number of activities or exercises or disciplines that are good because they help your guy grow in his relationship with God.

Although discussed previously in a narrative form, to get a clue to what Jesus thought our goal in making a disciple was to be, examine some of the verses that reference disciples.

Biblical Examples of Use of the Word "Disciple"

> A **disciple** is not above his teacher, nor a servant above his master. It is enough for the **Disciple** to be **like** his teacher, and the servant to be **like** his master. (Matt 10:24 RSV, Emphasis Added)

(***TEACHING MOMENT!)

> Simon Peter followed Jesus and so did another **disciple.** As this **disciple** was known to the high priest, he entered the court along with Jesus, while Peter stood outside at the door. So, the other **disciple**, who was known to the high priest, went out and spoke to the maid who kept the door, and brought Peter in. The maid who kept the door said to Peter "Are you not one of this man's **disciples**?" He said, "I am not." (Jn 18:15–16 RSV)

DISCIPLESHIP

(Setting: Jesus brought before the high priest just before His death)

> When Jesus saw His mother, and the **disciple** whom he loved standing near, He (Jesus) said to His Mother, "Woman, behold your son." Then he (Jesus) said to His **disciples**, "Behold, your mother!" And from that hour the **disciple** took her to his own home. (Jn 19:26 RSV)

(Setting: the crucifixion)

> After these days, we made ready and went up to Jerusalem. And some of His **disciples** from Caesare'a went with us, bringing us to the home of Mnason of Cyprus, an early **disciple**, with whom we would lodge. When we had come to Jerusalem, the brethren received us gladly. (Acts 21:16–17 RSV)
>
> Bind up the testimony, seal the teaching among my **disciples**. (Is 8:16 RSV)

It is interesting that the Old Testament only mentions the word **"disciple"** or **"disciples"** in one verse.

> Seeing the crowds, he went up on the mountain and when He sat down His **disciples** came to Him. And He opened His mouth, saying. (Mt 5:01 RSV)

Setting: Jesus gave "The Beatitudes." Note: Jesus had gotten away from the crowds and only His **disciples** were with him according to Matthew.

> Then the **disciples** of John came to Him, saying, "Why do the Pharisees fast but your **dis-**

DISCIPLESHIP

ciples do not fast?" And Jesus said to them, "Can the wedding guests mourn as long as the bridegroom is with them? The days will come when the Bridegroom will be taken away from them, and then they will fast." (Mt 9:14–5 RSV)

(***TEACHING MOMENT!)

    And He called to Him his 12 **disciples** and gave them authority over unclean spirits to cast the out, and to heal every disease and every infirmity. The names of the twelve are these. (Mt 10:01 RSV)

    Why do your **disciples** break the tradition of the Elders? They do not wash their hands before they eat. (Mt 15:02 NIV)

    Then the **disciples** came to Jesus in private and asked, "Why couldn't we drive it out?" (Mt 7:19 NIV)

    Then he returned to his **disciples** and found them sleeping. "Couldn't you men keep watch with me for one hour?" He asked Peter. But all this has all taken place that the writings of the prophets might be fulfilled then all the **disciples** deserted him and fled. (Mt 26:56 NIV)

    Go therefore and make d**isciples** of all nations, baptizing them in the name of the Father and of the Son and of the Holy Spirit., teaching them to observe all that I have commanded you, and lo, I am with you always, to the end of the age. (Mt 28:19–20 RSV)

    Now Jesus learned that the Pharisees had heard that he was gaining and baptizing more than John although in fact it was not Jesus who baptized, but his **Disciples**. So, he left Judea and went back once more to Galilee. (Jn 4:1–3 NIV)

From this time many of his **disciples** turned back and no longer followed him. (Jn 6:66 NIV)

To the Jews who believed him, Jesus said, "If you hold to my teaching, you are really my **disciples**. Then you will know the truth and the truth will set you free." (Jn 8:31–32 NIV)

At first his **disciples** did not understand all this. Only after Jesus was glorified did they realize that these things had been written about him and that these things had been done to him. (Jn 12:16 NIV)

Then Jesus's **disciples** said, "Now you are speaking clearly without figures of speech. Now we can see that you know all things and that you do not even need to have anyone ask you questions. This makes us believe that you came from God." (Jn 16:29–30 NIV)

Now Judas, who betrayed him, knew the place because he met there with his **disciples**. So Judas came to the garden, guiding a detachment of soldiers and some officials from the chief priests and the Pharisees. They were carrying torches, lanterns, and weapons. (Jn 18:2–4 NIV)

In those days when the number of **disciples** was increasing, the Hellenistic Jews among them complained against the Hebraic Jews because their widows were being overlooked in the daily distribution of food. So, the Twelve gathered all the **disciples** together and said, "It would not be right for us to neglect the ministry of the word of God to wait on tables. Brothers and sisters, choose seven men among you who are to be full of the Spirit and wisdom. We will turn this responsibility over to them and will give our attention to prayer and the ministry of the word." This proposal pleased the whole group.

They chose Stephen, a man full of faith and of the Holy Spirit, also Philip, Proch'orus, Micanor, Timon, Par'menas, and Nicola'us from Antioch, a convert to Judaism. They presented these men to the apostles, who prayed and laid their hands on them. So, the word of God spread. The number of **disciples** in Jerusalem increased rapidly, and a large number of priests became obedient to the faith. (Acts 6:1–7 NIV)

(TEACHING MOMENT)

Then Barnabas went to Tarsus to look for Saul, and when he found him, he brought him to Antioch. So, for a whole year, Barnabas and Saul met with the church and taught great numbers of people. The **disciples** were called Christians first at Antioch. (Acts 11:25–26 NIV)

Some of the **disciples** from Caesare'a accompanied us and brought us to the home of Mnason, where we were to stay. He was a man of Cyprus and one of the early **disciples**. (Acts 21:16 NIV)

"Of All Nations"

This part of Jesus's marching orders is rarely discussed and often overlooked, BUT it would not have gone unnoticed by His disciples!

Jesus was talking to His guys, who all happened to be Jewish. So when Jesus said, "Make disciples of ALL nations," the guys would have taken notice and might actually have looked around at each other, thinking or muttering, "THEM, we have to go out and make disciples of THEM!"

Jesus was talking about making disciples of NOT just the Jews but EVERYONE! There is no discussion of what the disciples thought of this part of the instruction, but they had to be thinking about it.

DISCIPLESHIP

Put your first disciple's hat on, go back to that moment and realize what this conceivably meant to each of them!

It is important to note here that this concept of ALL nations means a lot to those out in the mission field. They are determined (!) to play the part they are called to: to make disciples of ALL nations. To some friends of mine, that means East Africa!

To two other dear friends of mine, Rev. Charles (Charlie) and his wife, Phyllis Hardie, it was a lifetime commitment to bring the Good News of Christ to all nations, spending nineteen years in Taiwan and ending with thirteen years in Siberia (near Novosibirsk). I remember an email I received from Charlie describing his taking the Gospel to the farthermost reaches of Northern Siberia—no roads, only could be reached by boat, and him struggling to bring the gospel, who were so far removed from civilization, they lived off just berries and fish.

But Charlie was so in love with Jesus, he felt compelled to share the Good News everywhere he went. When they came by Seattle at the end of their missions, we went to the Locks, where ships transition from sea level to lake (Washington) level. Even there as Sue, Phyllis, and I looked at the salmon jumping up the ladders, Charlie felt compelled to strike up a conversation with an older gentleman to make sure he knew where he'd be going when he left this world. THAT was their passion.

At a men's ministry meeting of about twenty guys at a Denny's restaurant in the Bay Area of California, the pastor asked me directly, "So what do you think an evangelist looks like?"

This one was easy for me: "It's someone who almost cries when he walks into a restaurant like this, thinking one person in here might not know Jesus and might never know how much He loved and loves us."

So yes, the little word "all" the nations means everything to some, something different to others. So where is your all nations? It might be right where you are!

In reviewing my notes, I discovered several slightly different accounts of what Jesus said on it and what each did and did

DISCIPLESHIP

not include. Matthew, Mark, AND Luke account virtually the same message:

> Therefore go and <u>make disciples of all nations</u>, baptizing them…and teaching them obey everything I have commanded you. (**Matt 28:19–20** NIV) (which I probably have already quoted ten times in this book)

> Go into the world and <u>preach the good news to all creation</u>, Whoever believes and is baptized will be saved, but whoever does not believe will be condemned. (**Mark 16:15–16** NIV)

Note the subtle differences:

- Matthew understood this to mean we were to go into ALL the nations and make Disciples whereas Mark understood Jesus to mean preach and baptize.
- Mark does not address "go and make disciples."

> And repentance and forgiveness will be preached in His name <u>to all the nations</u> beginning at Jerusalem. (**Luke 24:47** NIV)

Again, Luke's account differs slightly: emphasizes preaching repentance and forgiveness. BTW, the word "repentance" means a turning away from sin. Hey, sometimes you cannot do this turning away by yourself, BUT bring it to God in prayer and tell Him something like, "Take this away from me!" and He will be faithful to help you. Trust me. I know about this one.

So how do we reconcile these three versions of what Jesus last words were:

- Do they contradict one another or

- Do they each fill in more detail of what and how they were to do it?

To me, it is clear:

- First comes the preaching, the sharing of the good news of eternal life through Christ, but with the proviso that this includes a willingness to repent (turn away from your sins) and forgive others.
- The disciples were to not keep this to themselves (the Jews), but they clearly understood, Christ was going to die for ALL of mankind, and to take this good news to the furthermost reaches of creation.
- Then comes the baptism, signifying you are a new thing as in a rebirth. Baptizing is a kind of cleansing: out with the old and the bad and in with God!
- Then he gets to "make disciples"; his guys knew what that meant, not just teaching, but emulating the disciple maker and carrying it on and on.
- The disciples were to "teach" them to OBEY what Jesus had COMMANDED them namely 1) love God completely and 2) to love one another.

That's it. That's what that itty-bitty word "ALL nations" includes.

"BAPTIZING THEM"

Jesus used the word "water" in a number of ways his disciples would understand.

To my simple brain, I have been taught that baptizing is "an OUTER sign of an INNER CHANGE."

The use by Christ of the water as a cleansing material was intentional.

Consider that following things Jesus DID (not said) at the last supper, just before and knowing full well he was about to be crucified:

> *Jesus, knowing that the Father had given all things into His hands and that He had come FROM God and was going TO God…rose from supper, laid aside his garments and girded himself with a towel. Then He poured water into a basin, and began to wash His Disciples feet, and to wipe them with the towel with which He was girded.* (John 13:3–5 RSV, Emphasis added)

Jesus went on to explain the significance of the example given by the washing of the feet: "He who has bathed does not need to wash, except for his feet, but he is clean all over; and you are clean" (John 13:10–12).

Jesus was not merely talking about the outward bathing or cleansing example. Jesus was talking about the cleansing that He brings to you by His indwelling in you.

Later, when He had finished, Jesus said (importantly) to them:

> *Do you know what I have done to you? You call me Teacher and Lord, and you are right, for so I am. If I then, your Lord and Teacher have washed your feet, you also ought to wash another's feet. For I have given you an example that you should do as I have done to you.* (John 13:12–15 RSV)

Is this clear to you? Jesus was giving you an example as to how to be a leader, a disciple maker. There needs to be this recognition of the cleansing only Christ can give; it is most evident when a person is baptized: the person has accepted Christ and he (or she) is a new person, a new creature.

Paul, in his second letter to the church in Corinth made it a little clearer: "Therefore, if anyone is in Christ, this person is a new creation: the old things passed away, new things have come" (2 Cor 5:17 NASB).

Jesus goes into some depth about this baptism, new beginning process. He described it as a rebirth. His Guys did not get it, at least at first. They said something like "How can I be reborn?"

Jesus answered them in John 3:5 NIV, "Very truly I tell you, no one can enter the kingdom of God unless they are born of water and spirit."

People have half-jokingly debated whether you have been dunked or sprinkled. John the Baptist said, before Christ appeared to him (roughly!), "I sprinkle you with water, but one is coming who will baptize you with the Spirit." The Bible also records that Jesus was baptized in the River Jordan (I believe) and records as he "came up out of the water."

Frankly, I don't think the medium matters; I do think the full-immersion baptism is just a more powerful statement: that the old has gone away and coming up out of the water, the person is a new creation.

I do not think baptism of a new child is what does it; the person has to be old enough to recognize he/she is making a choice and choosing Jesus. It IS significant in this kind of baptism that:

a) The parents are committing to bring up the child in the faith, and
b) The church is committing to help the parents do this. (There I go with this discipling as a process of coming alongside another Christian.)

It IS important to recognize that Jesus considered the baptism as important and actually necessary!

"Teaching Them"

Dawson Trotman, in the 1930s, came up with a concept of what the Christian's relationship might/should look like.

Mr. Trotman originated/founded an organization called the Navigators, which still is in existence today and operating out of Colorado.

What's neat about this organization is:

A) They taught me, and what I was taught in 1970 is surprisingly still applicable today!

B) They have provided neat tools that simplify and are easy to remember, like the Wheel, the essence of the well-balanced Christian disciple's life, and like the Word Hand, an easy to remember five ways of inculcating all this into your life.

What's really cool about this is they make these printable tools available to any of us, free of charge, AND instruct us by saying at the bottom of each, "THIS TOOL IS MEANT TO BE SHARED," and even give a link on the bottom where we can download a copy.

My aim here is to, in written form, list and describe some (but probably not all) of the ways an individual can come closer to God. It also provides a framework for a discipler to know the ways they can help another believer!

The Wheel is one of these tools and can be found at http://www.navlink.org/wheel.

The Word Hand can be found at http://www.navlink.org/word-hand.

I have also included a copy of the Word Hand printout in this book for your examination and, importantly, implementation!

Below is a copy from the Navigator's Website called the Wheel.

A relationship with God will/should include (to borrow from the Wheel word picture):

- Vertical relationship: This is His Word coming down to us in various forms. The Word, incorporating all or all we can, of the methods and ways to hear from God (hearing/reading/studying/praying).
- Vertical: These are our words to Him, like a little kid talking to his/her dad including prayer.
- Horizontal relationships: This used to be called evangelism, and I think now could be more characterized by the word "witnessing."
- Horizontal relationships: The second command says, "Love one another." It helps and builds up the church, the Body

DISCIPLESHIP

of Christ, by loving and encouraging one another, helping them in their time of need, okay, actually just sharing life with them. Many churches call this being in community.

Navigators Discipleship Tool

The Wheel diagram, created by Navigator founder Dawson Trotman in the 1930s, is a simple and effective way to visually explain the structure of a God-glorifying life. Sharing it can be as simple as drawing it on a napkin or notepad. The diagram challenges us to think deeply about how to be an obedient follower of Christ and each part represents a crucial component of a vibrant Christian life.

THE WHEEL

How you relate to yourself

THE CENTER HUB AND OUTER RIM

- **Christ:** Total surrender to Christ's authority and Lordship is not always a decision made right at conversion, but is a necessary act of the will. For the believer, the "old life" has gone and the new has come (2 Corinthians 5:77), because Christ has begun to dwell in us (Galatians 2:20). God creates within us the desire to do what He wants us to do in order to express His Lordship in our lives.

- **The Obedient Christian in Action:** Some acts of obedience to God are internal, such as attitudes, habits, motives, values and day-to-day thoughts. But even these eventually surface outwardly in our relationships with other people. Keeping His commands in obedience is our outward indication of inward health and love for Christ (John 74:27, Romans 72:1).

How you relate to God

THE VERTICAL SPOKES

- **The Word:** God uses His word to speak directly to us, revealing not only who He is, but how He calls us to live and interact with everyone around us (2 Timothy 3:76). This means an earnest personal intake of God's Word is essential for our spiritual health and growth (Joshua 1:8). As God speaks to us through the Scriptures, we learn how to obey Him and apply the gospel to every part of our lives. We also come to know Jesus personally and find He is worthy of our steadfast allegiance.

- **Prayer:** Prayer is the natural response to God as we hear Him speak through His Word. It is sharing our heart with the One who longs for our companionship and who cares about our concerns. Prayer not only trains our hearts and minds to know the power and glory of God, but also turns His ear towards action in our lives (John 75:7, Philippians 4:6-7).

How you relate to others

THE HORIZONTAL SPOKES

- **Fellowship:** God has directed Christians to build each other up through interdependence and loving relationships with each other (Hebrews 70:24-25). Gathering together as the Body of Christ draws God close around us as we praise Him and encourage one another (Matthew 18:20).

- **Witnessing:** God has given believers the joy and responsibility of telling the world about the good news of Christ's work on Earth (Matthew 4:79). In fact, sharing about His amazing grace is the natural overflow of a rich, vibrant life in Christ (Romans 7:16).

THIS TOOL IS MEANT TO BE SHARED. To download a copy visit navlink.org/wheel
The Wheel ©1976,(2016)by The Navigators. All rights reserved.

The wheel

A few words on Trotman's tool, the Wheel, that have impacted my life.

Christ IS the Hub.

As in any wheel, the wheel needs a hub.

If the hub, Christ, is not at the center of it all, of all life, then it's not balanced and is just words, it's just a life well lead. Also, if it's not in balance, the wheel will spin awkwardly, and necessarily, life will be difficult, relationships won't work, and you won't be in touch with God as much as if you had the vertical and horizontal spokes working properly.

We can be friendly or go through the prayer motions or hear the Word and not let it have a real impact on our life, it may look good, but it's just surface paint, just meaningless words or actions.

If going to different church functions to check off the fellowship box, unless it is Christ driven and centered, may make you look good and all clean, but real fellowship contains below the surface discussion and heartfelt encouragement.

The spokes

Over the years, I have taught the Wheel concept and pondered the topic of the balance of the various spokes in our life, and I still (!) have no conclusion on it BUT have concluded that the four equal appearing spokes does NOT mean that every hour of prayer time MUST BE met with an hour of witnessing. It's just that we need all four aspects in our daily lives in much is possible.

DISCIPLESHIP

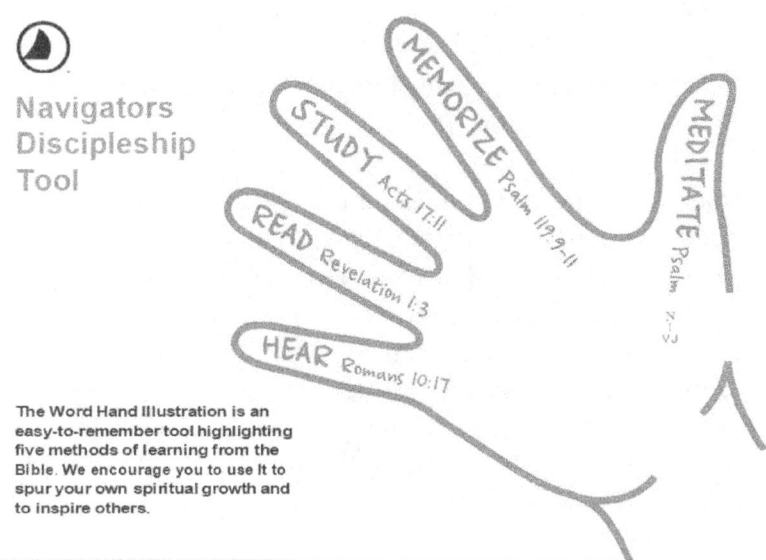

Navigators Discipleship Tool

The Word Hand Illustration is an easy-to-remember tool highlighting five methods of learning from the Bible. We encourage you to use it to spur your own spiritual growth and to inspire others.

THE WORD HAND

HEARING pastors and teachers teach from the Word provides fresh insight into the Scriptures. The weakest finger (the pinkie) represents hearing, because we retain only five percent of what we hear. *Romans 10:17*

READING gives us an overview of the Bible and is the foundation of a daily quiet time. This is represented by the ring finger. We generally retain 15 percent of what we read. *Revelation 1:3*

STUDYING the Scriptures deepens our convictions. It requires greater time and effort but results in increased knowledge of the Bible. Most people retain 35 percent of what they study. This is represented by the middle finger. *Acts 17:17*

MEMORIZING God's Word enables us to use Scripture, "the Sword of the Spirit" (Ephesians 6:17), to overcome temptations and to have verses readily available for ministering to others. The index finger, our strongest finger, represents memorization. We remember 100 percent of what we memorize if we consistently review it. *Psalm 119:9-71*

MEDITATION is the process that accompanies each of the other four methods of Scripture intake. This is why meditation is assigned to the thumb. Only the thumb can touch all the other four fingers. By meditating on God's Word as we hear, read, study, and memorize, we discover its transforming power at work in us. *Psalm 7:2-3*

 navigators

THIS TOOL IS MEANT TO BE SHARED. **To download a copy visit navlink.org/word-hand**

The remainder of this section includes more detail on each element:

- Reading the Word of God, and
- Studying the Word of God, and

- Quiet times / devotionals, and
- Meditating on God's Word, and
- Committing God's Word to your memory, and
- Prayer

Again, all and each of these is simply to bring you closer to God in your daily life and hear what he is actually saying. They are not meant to be a checklist nor that you aren't okay if you don't do them all, every single day. Don't let the devil make you feel that you are somehow failing as a Christian. (He WILL try! Trust me on this one!)

Another way to think of these tools (reading, studying, devotionals, prayer, etc.) is to think of them as simply ways to bring you closer to God and away from your old, sinful life. Graphically, I have come up with a chart. (Hey, I am an accountant—EVERY thing has to have a chart!)

The main thing here is to realize all of the tools I will talk to you about are not to do's, but merely different ways of talking to, learning about, and in general, bring you into a closer relationship with God. This is where your discipler/coach can help you and be there to explain things and, importantly, see how he goes about having and deepening a relationship with God.

DISCIPLESHIP

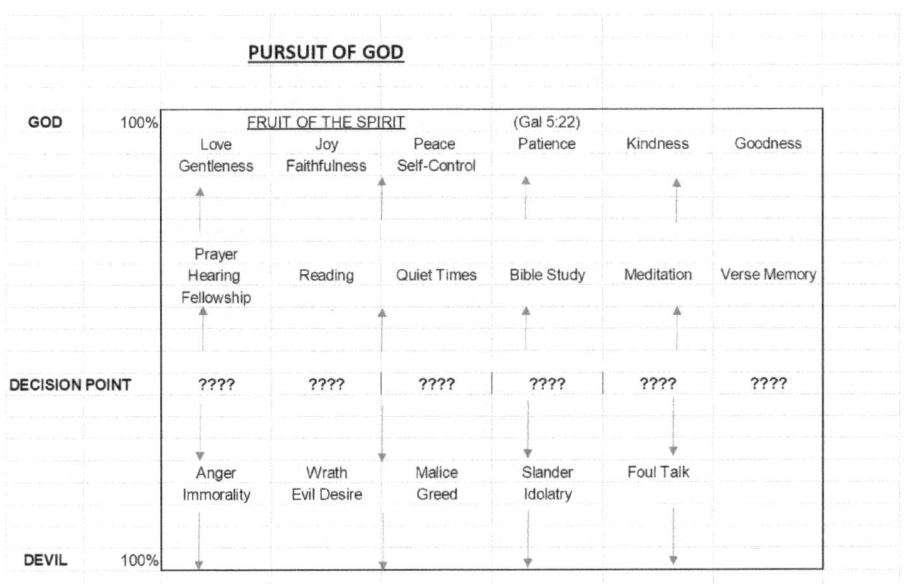

Fig 1.1

Fig 1.1 explained:

I included this graph to show you the reader a different way to look at all the disciplines that can be employed <u>to help us and our disciples grow closer to Christ.</u> This book is ALL about strengthening and deepening our relationship with Christ. All we can do should be about drawing ever closer to Christ.

Example: devotionals/quiet times

We set aside a time and find a quiet place. Why?

Is it so we can check off or count this as something we did to be a good Christian? No! We do it because we want to spend some time with Christ, where it's just Christ and me.

All of these disciplines are just "tools," methods, practices that bring us into His presence.

I have tried to show it in graphic form so one can see, the more we employ these tools, the closer we get to be with and get to know the Christ!

When we don't employ the tools, we sink downward toward evil thinking and behaving.

We don't have to or want to accumulate how many times per week we did one or more of these things, like if we get twenty-five points, we get a gold star! (Yes, it is amazing that I, as a CPA, did not give a weighted value to each thing you do or times you did it. LOL.)

I was asked once, "Does it COUNT as a quiet time if I sing to God in the shower?" The object is not how many times we get with God and the quality of the time doesn't matter, God knows the heart.

The more we get with God, stay in touch with Him, the more we experience what Paul talked about in Galatians 5:22–23 as the "fruit of the Spirit: love, joy, peace, patience, kindness, goodness, faithfulness, gentleness, self-control."

At each moment in time, we can ask ourselves and our disciples can ask themselves, "Am I moving TOWARD a closer walk with God or am I walking AWAY from God?" The graph shows the consequences of each choice we make.

1. Reading the Bible

This practice has always been hard for me. Why? Because it takes time, and I am a busy man! LOL. Seriously, the benefits are immense:

- By reading the Old Testament, you get context: how did we get here?
- When Jesus speaks of the Law, you know where that comes from: Jewish Law.
- There are a lot of promises in the Old Testament, some for us and some for all people that were fulfilled in Jesus.

The sixty-six books of the Bible are not just a folder full of all the scrolls they could find, it is all of God's Word, nothing more and nothing less. If you read it, you will see how it all hangs together.

There are no conflicting stories, just one thread that permeates the whole book, and that is God's Love for Us—you and me! BTW, if you run into seemingly conflicting or difficult passages, there is a book that goes into each one of these and explains each.

DISCIPLESHIP

<u>*Difficulties in the Bible: Alleged Errors and Contradictions*</u> by R. A. Torrey, Moody Books, Chicago.

The reasons for reading the Bible are obvious:

It is God's word to us in total, so if we want to get to know Him better, what better way to get to know Him, but to read of Him and His works and His leading and protecting us down through the ages? There are points where God said, "Let's start over." Examples:

- Remember Noah and the flood and how He took one family to start over?
- Remember Sodom and Gomorrah and how He took one family out of there to start over?

Okay, here are some things that help in the process:

Read the Bible all the way through in one year or in seven months.

- The Internet is full of programs, which break down a large book (!) into manageable readable chunks.
- I prefer a plan that takes it from the beginning and goes through to the end. Some break up the Bible, reading at three or four different starting points. Personally, I find that confusing for my little brain; you don't have to remember where you were in each of the four sections and what was going on. However, perhaps that works for you. I just encourage you to do it: read His Word.
- Also, importantly, the Bible, as constructed, takes this world and the universe for that matter from beginning ("In the beginning") and ends with the last book, Revelation, which tells of the end of all time.

Take time out for God. If you have to schedule an appointment with God or block out a portion of each day to read the Bible, then set aside a specific place—the couch early in the morning or at the office late at night—when there are no distractions.

I will remind you time and time again: PLEASE don't make this a task you gotta do. You pursue God as a joy with an attitude of gratitude. A habit helps you get there more often, but PLEASE don't ever let the outlined schedule outweigh the love for Him.

2. *Studying the Bible*

This is the easiest part for me to talk to you about! For me, it's the most fun! I love to read and study the Word of God; sometimes, it just blows me away!

Example: Just today, from a song I heard where at the end, this little child quotes some verses from Isaiah 41:

> *The Lord God is the everlasting God, the Creator of the ends of the earth… He (God!) does not faint or grow weary* **<u>(the depth of) His understanding is unsearchable.</u>** (Is 41:28 RSV, Emphasis added)

> <u>*But they who wait for the Lord shall renew their strength, they shall mount up with wings of eagles, they shall run and not be weary, they shall walk and not faint.*</u> (Is 41:31 RSV)

Those verses, especially Isaiah 41:31, were heard and learned and then relied on by me fifty years ago (!) to get me through jump school at Fort Benning where we'd run three miles before breakfast. Yes, God gave me strength then, and eventually, I got my "wings."

Today though, I heard Him (God) bring to my little brain—a part I had never focused on in fifty years! <u>*"The depth of His understanding is unsearchable!"*</u> (Emphasis added)

Do you see how active and alive God's word can be? By His word, I grew strong fifty years ago, and then today, those same exact verses opened up my heart, in a new and different way. He understands me and what I am going through physically, how at nights I am in pain often and can't sleep till daylight, and understands what I am wrestling with internally and personally. It says basically NO ONE understands me better than Him and He knows ALL of me.

As I was sitting on the deck, this concept of Him understanding me better than I ever could really hit me.

Many times I have heard His still, small voice, but none so clearly and so TIMELY as the one today!

Let the Word of God so permeate YOUR life. He's there always!

Sorry, I diverge!

It's also good to do Bible studies either in a group or with your discipler. He can shed light on various aspects on whatever you are studying. Doing it with someone else—you get their perspective or how at some point this or that verse affected them. There is this aspect of the Word which is remarkably interesting:

Logos: there is the written Word, a "divine wisdom manifest in the creation, government, and redemption of the world," often identified with the second person of the Trinity. It often means an appeal to logic, meaning it is to appeal to the audience's reason or logic. This is good for knowledge and context.

Rhema: there is this active Word, where the Word is actually alive and can penetrate you in unbelievable ways. This same Word which IS Christ can be active in today's world right now! That action IS the Holy Spirit, which lives in every believer ALL THE TIME! Wow!

His Word is alive!

Hebrews 4:12 (NIV) says, "For the Word of God is alive and active. Sharper than any double-edged sword, it penetrates even to dividing soul and spirit, joints, and marrow. It judges the thoughts and attitudes of the heart."

All scripture is good! Read the following anew:

Second Timothy 3:16 NIV says, "All scripture is God breathed and is useful for teaching, rebuking, correcting, and training in righteousness, so that the servant of God may be thoroughly equipped for every good work."

Lastly, from a version of the Bible called *The Message*, something powerful comes out in 1 Corinthians 3:16, where Paul says, "You realize, don't you, that you are the temple of God, and God himself is present in you?" God is actually in us—available to all of us—all the time.

Do you want to endeavor to be holy and righteous?
Read and study the Bible.

3. Study books of the Bible

If you want to study ONE book in the Bible, I encourage you to get a guidebook, either at a Christian bookstore or one online.

The reason is when you have a guidebook, you learn a lot more or learn things you never knew! Second, study with someone. I can't tell you all the times that my discipler/mentor has taught me new things from passages I have read maybe fifty times!

4. Topical studies

Topical studies are where you hone in and try to really understand a person of the Bible or a phrase in the Bible.

There are books on, say, the life of Paul for example.

I have also found a couple of resources invaluable, including:

- **Nave's Topical Bible** where, for example, it gives numerous verses focusing on (organized alphabetically) a specific word like "chastity" or "heaven."
- **"Treasury of Scripture Knowledge"** was given to me by my first discipler, Lt. Mike Welch, on the occasion of my birthday, January 12, 1970. My copy is now tattered and worn, but still oh so useful!

    It also has a reference at the bottom to 1 Thessalonians 2:8 RSV, *"So, being affectionately desirous of you, we were ready to share with you not only the gospel of God, but also our own selves, because you had become very dear to us."* That my friends was and is "Discipleship."
- **Haley's Bible Handbook.** This is a book I got more recently which is organized by the books of the Bible and is very useful in describing the times it was written and has

many pictures of places, maps of that part of the world at the time that book was written. This is very useful to get a mental picture when the Bible says, "And he journeyed from ____ to ____" and shows graphically how far it was to walk (no rapid transit was available!) from their starting point to the next destination.

You will also notice the same event is recorded in another Gospel with almost identical wording. The books of Matthew, Mark, and Luke are very similar, and there are books that compare and contrast the same stories written from different viewpoints. It is also useful if you want to see if, where, or of how a particular verse is repeated in another of the gospels. These are called the Synoptic Gospels, but I like to think of each one of these three as the reports from three reporters reporting in different newspapers. Have you noticed the same account is often repeated in another gospel? I find it very compelling in believing and having faith that the gospel, the Good News of Jesus Christ is real and accurate and backed up by more than one source!

- **Concordance.** Most Bibles have what is called a concordance, and it is where you can find either a word or a phrase or concept, which may shed light on a particular verse where it does not make sense to you, possibly because you don't know that particular part of Jewish history or events.

  This is immensely useful! Example: The verse I referenced above, Isaiah 40:29, uses the word "strength." In the concordance in my Bible, it gives twenty-one additional citings where that word is used.

  Also, most Bibles, on the outer or inner margins, where else that verse or its concept can be found elsewhere in the Bible.

Do you see how fun this can be—to explore, gain context, and really understand what a verse or passage means?

Bible study is not meant solely for monks in some monastery. The Word of God is meant to be read and understood by guys like you and me!

The Word is alive and active!

Have fun exploring the depths of His Word!

5. *Quiet times / devotionals*

Quiet time = getting alone with God
Why?

With our busy lives, we sometimes get overwhelmed by all the daily to-do's and people coming at us with questions or the need for decisions and the noise of texts, emails, Tweets, Facebook posts, Zoom calls, and on and on. We get so busy, sometimes, we simply don't know which way to turn or which "thing" to do next!

In crises, we hurriedly ask God for help and wonder, "Why am I not hearing from God on how I should handle the current mess I am in," whether it's mental or physical or even spiritual?

- God, can you get me out of this mess or condition?
- God, what am I supposed to do with my job? Their values/decisions don't line up with what I really believe? Should I just quit?
- God, is this the woman for me?
- God, can you give me a sign on which way I should go?

Do any of this sound familiar?

Well, early on in my experience as a Christian, I learned to get (very!) alone with God where I can quiet myself and shut out all those competing voices in my head. I call it quiet time. (Some call it devotionals.)

Practical steps to implementing a quiet time:

This is real, practical stuff you can implement right now, today, or early tomorrow morning. I will explain the why's for each step in a minute.

DISCIPLESHIP

Simply put:

1. Find and go to a place that is quiet where you won't be interrupted.
2. Read some pre-appointed scripture; maybe read it several times.
3. Write down what you are feeling, hearing, in some kind of a journal."
4. Pray about what you learned or what you heard (might be God's instructions) or what you felt. Hey, it's YOUR journal; write down what you felt that day.
5. Try to extract something practical that applies to just you.
6. Now, you can go about your day!

Hint: You will most likely find what I have that "The day goes better after you've had your DQT!" (daily quiet time).

Get quiet

With all the hustle and bustle in our lives, it's almost impossible to really get some peace, even at home sometimes. I like to find a place where I can drive to and get out and walk to a bench or maybe just stop the car and shut off the car AND the radio! (LOL.) (Just getting quiet in your car is really helpful, if it's like 10 degrees outside!)

My first discipler, Mike, used to drive with me out to a lake—just south of the lake near the Laredo Air Force Base—where we would start our day, VERY early in the day before the busy-ness of the day started. I can still remember those times. Although raised in a churchgoing family and as a confirmed Lutheran, I didn't really know much about the Bible, and I certainly did not know the verses could come alive for me!

Sometimes, I have gone/driven with a disciple, and we'd go to a baseball field and sit in the bleachers. On the way there, we would catch up on stuff. Then we go to a bleacher seat, and we would start out with a prayer to God to help us get quiet before Him, to shut out the noise.

We'd pause...then we'd begin.

Sometimes, when I travel, I find a park or (in California) find a grove of trees I can walk into and be alone with God. Sometimes, these quiet times don't come with the luxury of being able to write down what you hear or feel.

When talking or teaching about what I call quiet time alone with God, a dear lady, an elder actually, asked me, "Does it COUNT if I sing songs to God in the morning while I shower?" like it would give her five points and if she only got XX number of points for the day, it would satisfy God.

Do we really think God didn't like her singing praise to Him?

I just treasure that time! Time to take maybe fifteen to twenty, sometimes thirty, minutes alone with God. It frequently amazes me that God will meet me there! Here is the God that created the whole freaking universe, and He wants (relishes I think!) to spend some time with little, old me!

You too can also enjoy that unique, uplifting, joy-filled, instructive, or constructive time with God!

The Word of God

The scripture tells us: *"All scripture is inspired (*) <u>and is useful</u> for teaching, for reproof (**), for correction, and for training in righteousness, that the man of God me complete (***), equipped for every good work"* (2 Tim 3:16 RSV).

(*) The NIV translates "inspired" to be more on the order of "God-breathed." I like that translation; it hits me that the Word of God is actually alive and active like God himself has breathed life into that Word!

(**) "Reproof" is a word that is very similar to "correction," but is almost a statement of disapproval as in "rebuking," but in this setting, it is more akin to a "kind and gentle correction." I think God usually (or almost always) works in this kinder and gentler mode. Matthew records Jesus saying, *"Take my yoke upon you, and learn from me, for **I am gentle and lowly in heart**, <u>**and you will find rest**</u> for your souls"* (Matt 11:29 RSV).

In case you still have doubts about working in you and how He does it, the Bible gives us some welcomed assurance:

*** Philippians 1:6 NASB says, "For I am confident of this very thing, that He who began a good work in you will perfect (***) it until the day of Jesus Christ."

(***) NIV translates the word "perfect" as meaning Jesus will bring it to completion "thoroughly complete," as in perfectly complete.

That is so reassuring!

I have been reproofed by pastors over the years and one in particular. I can know his words are of God by the manner it was delivered, gently and thoughtfully delivered with the love of a merciful God. This pastor could have torn into me and could have told me, "Gar, you are WAY off base here!" but no, he starts off by saying, "Gar, I humbly submit the following suggestions."

How do you think that second version, this pastor's response, was received? When I think back on it, I am almost in tears as I write this; it was so on point, yet the truth was spoken in love! That, my friends, is God's voice to the point, but spoken to me so I respond and am humbled by the love in which it is delivered. *"For God so **loved** the world."*

I think we sometimes we forget that God usually speaks to us through scripture. So the Bible, the Word of God, is or can be actually alive!

In the Greek, there are a couple of words used to describe the Word of God:

- "Logos" meaning the literal word of God. The truth, a written record.
- "Rhema" meaning the Word can be alive!

So use scripture in any quiet time/devotional you have; let God speak to you in those moments through His Word.

Listen to the following, attributed by many as coming from Paul:

> <u>For the Word of God is living and active</u>, *sharper than any two-edged sword, piercing ("penetrates" NIV) to the division of soul and spirit, of joints and marrow, and discerning ("judges" NIV) the thoughts and intentions of the heart.* (Heb 4:12 RSV)

On reflecting on this crucial verse, I am struck by its inclusion JUST after the author talks about this rest that comes in a relationship with Christ. This affirms the inclusion in my earlier writing, that Jesus taught us we'd find rest for our souls in Him.

Write It Down!

Over the years, I have found many ways and tools that helped me to journal the words or messages I heard during my quiet time. For now, just get any blank journal or a tablet of paper and dwell on a verse or some verses that you heard on Sunday and then write down your thoughts or what you think you hear.

Be assured, He will meet you there.

> *Draw near to God and He will draw close to you.* (Jas 4:8 RSV)

> *For we do not have a High Priest who is unable to sympathized with our weaknesses, but we have one who has been tempted in every way, just as we are yet, without sin. <u>Let us then approach the throne of grace with confidence</u>, so that we may receive mercy and find grace to help us in our time of need.* (Heb 4:16 NIV, Emphasis added)

> *And since we have a great Priest over the house of God. <u>Let us draw near to God</u> with a sincere*

> *heart in full assurance of faith, having our hearts sprinkled to cleanse us from a guilty conscience and having our bodies washed with pure water.* (Heb 10:21–22 NIV)

I have used several journals over the years including simple paperback journals that have a verse or verses for that day. A place for some notes and almost always a place for application: how is this going to change my life or answer my question? This is not book learning—these are life-changing encounters!

Check out a few kinds and publishers of daily quiet time journals. As an example, check out the classic devotional: *My Utmost for His Highest* by Oswald Chambers. Also, the Navigators have some very useful tools in this area. There are also online tools to record what you hear or feel from your devotionals; however, I am old-school. I like to write it down and (maybe) scratch through what I just wrote down, as I get closer to writing what is really hitting me that morning. Then, when I revisit it later in the day, I will remember the travails I went through to express what was really on my heart.

As hinted at above, there are some elements that help me, so open up a couple of journals and pick a format that suits you.

- Each day should have a verse or verses that draw you into His Word. God usually will speak to you through His Word. God may use others to speak to you, especially when you need to be jarred back to your senses (!), but generally, it's His Word.
- Some versions have a commentary on the verse. Some I like, as they speak in plain English; some I do not like, as they may be too preachy or just intellectual. Find one you are comfortable with and want to get started on right away; that's the best way to know this one is right for you.
- Personally, I don't like dated ones: one for each day of the year. I am human, and if I miss a day here or there, I feel guilty because that day will be forever blank.

- I always look for one that has space designed for application. This, for me, is where change happens.
- I personally don't like printed prayers. I want to thank Him on my own or let Him know I agree with Him or ask His help in understanding what it is He is trying to tell me or get me to do. These prayers are some of my most intimate exchanges with God. I feel like I can tell Him: "Hey, God, I am not there yet. Help my unbelief!"

<u>God says to us today, just as he did to Abram</u> as recorded in the very first book of the Bible: *"When Abram was ninety-nine years old, the Lord appeared to him and said, <u>'I am God Almighty; walk before me and be blameless'"</u>* (Gen 17:1 NIV).

"The Daily Kairos Journal"

One tool I have heard of but have not tried is called a <u>*Daily Kairos Journal,*</u> and I am considering trying one out. One reviewer wrote, "Not only does it drive my daily engagement (with God). It has a section to help me see the big picture of what I have been learning over the week. The quality of the notebook is really nice, and I like that it has the bookmarks for the day and the weekly entries."

There are a lot of online tools/apps for recording what happens/what you learned and takeaways available.

Back to my original premise, I am not a man of a lot of discipline, i.e., I hate gotta-do's. That feeling of obligation actually drove me away from God for years.

Rather, I now approach my life with God on what I call a heart approach, which is I respond to His leading to pray or be nice to some undeserving person or simply say, "I am sorry for ___" because He moves my heart, and if I respond to these nudges, I draw closer and closer to Him, not physically, but with this kind of relationship, the more and more I seek or respond to His leading/nudges, the happier/fulfilled I feel.

There are a number of sources to find devotionals online and in bookstores including the following, just to name a few:

- *The Upper Room*: with verse(s) and a provoking story, thought, or perspective on that verse.
- *My Utmost for His Highest*, a classic/book by Oswald Chambers.

This one has a verse, a commentary, AND a place to write some notes or takeaways. This only thing I don't like is it's dated: it has a devotional for every single day of the year, so if I miss one, I tend to feel guilty, like I didn't measure up! Hey, I am just human!

6. Meditating on His Word

Let me tell you a story of what it means to dwell on, okay, meditate on for more than a few seconds or minutes.

First some backdrop info: A couple who lived in San Jose California and basically gave up their lives to a church plant in Fremont, California.

When the church in San Jose asked them and one other couple to help sponsor a church plant in Fremont, they both came on board. Now this sponsorship was not a "give some money and get your name on a plaque" type sponsorship! For twenty or maybe thirty years (!), they drove up from San Jose to help the pastor start this church.

That entailed a fairly lengthy drive every Sunday but also included this man volunteering his time, which meant more drives from San Jose to Fremont, on a regular basis. He served as an elder in this RCA (Reformed Church in America), which meant more time and more drives. She was part of the church choir, meaning more trips, more time.

This man was a mature and Godly man, the man you'd like to emulate.

His wife was a graceful, God-loving woman, also an elder, who modeled for us what it means to be a Godly woman with her life and how she led women's studies in their home. They didn't have to do all this: the husband had a successful business in San Jose, California

One horrible night, they were T-boned in their car by the driver of another car who had run a red light. This was not a fender bender! The crash pinned the wife against her husband, causing significant and serious injuries to both. The crash also pinned the driver against the metal door.

His life, for some time, was in serious jeopardy!

This incident still gives me chills, even now, when I think back on that time, not knowing if they were going to survive.

I wanted to pray for them. I did.

But I wanted God's assurance that they'd be okay.

Somehow, I returned to a verse I had memorized some time ago. Jesus said, ***"If you abide in me and my words abide in you, ask whatever you will, and it shall be done for you"*** (Jn 15:7 RSV).

(BTW, this promise follows some pretty stern warnings from Jesus to His guys: *"If a man does not abide in me, he is cast forth as a branch and withers; and the branches are gathered, thrown into the fire, and burned"* (Jn 15:6 RSV)).

So I thought on this verse a lot—I mean, a LOT!

It consumed me totally to know what it really meant.

- What did it mean, "If you ABIDE in ME"?
- What does it mean, "AND my words ABIDE in YOU"?
- That word "abide" is in there twice! Why?
- Is it just the *Merriam-Webster* definition (to bear patiently, to endure without yielding, to accept without objection)?
- Or does it mean as in the Thesaurus more like: dwell, hang around, remain, stay, stick around, to continue to be in a place for a significant amount of time?
- What did Jesus mean when He said, "ABIDE"?

Let me be very clear, I do not, in any way, take any credit for my thinking and meditating on these words or any credit for any prayers I offered up on the outcome. To God be the glory!

They both survived and recovered. (Thanks God!)

My **sole** purpose in going through this was to emphasize how we can think on and meditate on Jesus's simple yet clear command to love God.

Meditating on this one concept of loving God with all your strength, soul, and mind can and should occupy our thinking for the rest of our lives. I think the whole of a Christian's life can be boiled down into these two commands: love God and love one another.

Lastly, Paul adds a beautiful thing that can change our lives. He says:

> *Finally brethren,*
> *whatever is true,*
> *whatever is honorable,*
> *whatever is just,*
> *whatever is pure,*
> *whatever is lovely,*
> *whatever is gracious,*
> *if there is any excellence,*
> *if there is anything worthy of praise,*
> **think about these things.** (Phil 4:8 RSV)

It is that simple, and yet that is so full!

Now, as an exercise, go back and think each and every one of those encouragements. Go ahead! This book will wait for you!

Think of something that is true or, maybe easier, something that is honorable.

Do you see how meditating on each part of this verse can be helpful/useful?

Are you kinda getting it?

7. Commit His Words to your memory

When you are memorizing verses, you are in effect meditating on His Word. It sounds like a daunting task to memorize!

Try this; memorize the following verse: 1 Thessalonians 5:16 RSV, *"Pray constantly."*

There you have it. You have committed that to memory by just memorizing two words. Memorize the verse and where it came from (1 Thess 5:16) and you have it.

Verse memory is a different kind of meditation. I had a rather extensive collection of verses that I had memorized. When I walked away, I lost the habit and the box that contained the verse memory cards and in it all my verses. I am getting back into that habit.

Although this almost sounds like a gotta-do or a hard task, it's not.

There is value in using this tool:

1. In effect, you are meditating on His Word, which draws you closer to Him, and
2. You will focus on one verse or even just one word that was said, and
3. You keep His Word right in front of you, and
4. Certain verses will be with you and remind you (some forever).

Example: assurance of salvation in Psalm 119:11, *"Thy words have I Hid in my heart that I might not sin against thee" (KJV)*.

That verse kind of sums it all up: You keep His Word in front of you all the time. If you work at it in certain situations, your mind will go to wherever you "stashed" that verse in your brain, so you can recall it when needed!

In effect, then you are both memorizing AND meditating!

Cool concept, right?

The Navigators put out a quick reference guide with concrete but easy to follow instructions. A printable version of that follows.

DISCIPLESHIP

How to Memorize Scripture:

From its beginnings, The Navigators has encouraged Bible memorization as an important tool for spiritual growth. NavPress created the Topical Memory System with verse packs that The Navigators has incorporated in its ministry strategy since its founder Dawson Trotman used verse cards with sailors. The ministry has developed packets of verse cards to enable people to learn verses that will help them share their faith and become more like Christ. These cards are grouped by subject or "topic" and comprise what we call the Topical Memory System. This article references these topics in its suggestions for effective memorization. Find out more on the Topical Memory System here, or go to navigators.org/tms.

As you start to memorize a verse...

- Read in your Bible the context of each verse you memorize.
- Try to gain a clear understanding of what each verse actually means. You may want to read the verse in other Bible translations or paraphrases or perhaps consult a commentary-after you've done your personal study!

DISCIPLESHIP

HOW TO MEMORIZE SCRIPTURE
A SIMPLE , EASY BIBLE MEMORY SYSTEM

- Read the verse through several times thoughtfully, aloud or in a whisper. This will help you grasp the verse as a whole. Each time you read it, say the topic, reference, verse, and then the reference again.
- Discuss the verse with God in prayer, and continue to seek His help for success in Scripture memory.

While you are memorizing the verse...

- Work on saying the verse aloud as much as possible.
- Learn the topic and reference first.
- After learning the topic and reference, learn the first phrase of the verse. Once you have learned the topic, reference, and the first phrase and have repeated them several times, continue adding more phrases after you can quote correctly what you have already learned.
- Think about how the verse applies to you and your daily circumstances. Always include the topic and reference as part of the verse as you learn and review it.

After you can quote correctly the topic, reference, verse, and reference again...

- Writing the verse out can be helpful. This deepens the impression in your mind.
- Find a friend to check you on the verse. Better yet, memorize together! Review the verse immediately after learning it, and repeat it frequently in the next few days. This is crucial for fixing the verse firmly in your mind because of the tendency to forget something recently learned.
- Review! Review! Review! Repetition is the best way to engrave the verses on your memory.

navigators.org

DISCIPLESHIP

8. What gives us the right to pray?

One of the important concepts in the story of Jesus is what He did in His death. In dying to pay the price for our sins, by Christ's dying, Christ also enabled us to speak with God and have the relationship.

Prior to Jesus's death, only a priest could go into the inner temple, the Holy of Holies. As I understand it, this barrier was signified by an actual curtain, indicating to all, you cannot go further, you cannot get closer to God. You could not make a sacrifice directly to God to atone (pay the price for) or make up for your sins. You were separated from God. Recall my writing about that unspeakable word "sin." This had gone on for more than a thousand years.

As Christ died, the barrier between us and talking with and being with God was removed. Matthew explains it this way: that just Jesus cried out in a loud voice and His "soul was released." At that very moment, the barrier to the inner temple was opened.

> *And behold, the curtain of the temple was torn in two, from top to bottom; and the earth shook, and the rocks were split. (Matt 27:51 RSV)*

This act was so very important to us in a very, very practical way!

We can now approach God.

Additionally, and not to be forgotten, Jesus now sits at the right hand of God, interceding for us.

> *Likewise the Spirit help with us in our weakness, for we do not know how to pray as we ought. But the Spirit himself intercedes for us* **with sighs (other versions "groans") too deep for words**.
> (Rom 8:26, 28 RSV)

Jesus is there when we pray, however new we are to praying.

In fact, my wife, after she experienced her conversion, started her prayers with "Hi, God, it's me again!" Now she is in prayer almost the entire day when she walks into her office, when she is in meetings, and she has a surrender prayer taped to her laptop as a constant reminder.

Teach your disciples to come to God simply, like a child.

I believe God will smile, as a good Father would to talk with and spend time with His child, you. It brings me to tears when I think that the God of the whole universe will stop (if I will stop) and sit with and listen to me, as a good Father just loves to sit and listen to his kids.

In coaching a disciple, we need to not only teach them how to pray, we need to pray <u>with</u> them, modeling Jesus's prayers, modeling what it looks like to pray earnestly.

Be aware and make your disciples aware: SIN HINDERS PRAYER.

God cannot look on sin (just disregard it!), so if you want to talk to God, go to God, laying it all out there on the table. Be flat-out honest. Why?

He knows everything about you anyway!

Hmmm.

Consider that one for a moment!

9. How should we pray?

The apostle Matthew lays it all out there in Matthew 6:5–9 and records what Jesus taught His disciples. In Luke's remarkably similar version of the event, Luke records it as happening as follows:

> <u>He (Jesus) was praying in a certain location, and when He ceased, one of His Disciples said to Him, "Lord teach us to pray, as John taught his Disciples."</u> (Luke 11:1–4 RSV)

DISCIPLESHIP

Both versions teach almost the same exact words and reveal the method of how we should pray.

- Be alone.

    And after he had dismissed the crowds. He (Jesus) went up onto the hills, by Himself, to pray. (Matt 14:23 RSV)

    And when you pray, you must not be like the hypocrites; for they love to stand and pray in the synagogues and at the street corners, that they may be seen by men. Truly, I say to you, they have their reward. But, when you pray, go into your room, and shut the door and pray to your Father who is in secret; and your Father who sees in secret will reward you.
    And in praying do not heap up empty phrases as the Gentiles do; for they think that they will be heard for their many words. Do not be like them, for your Father knows what you need before you ask Him. (Matt 6:5–9 RSV)

- Pray with boldness!

    For we have not a high priest who is unable to sympathize with our weakness, but one who, in every respect, has been tempted as we are, yet, without sinning. **Let us then with confidence draw near to the throne of grace**, *that we may receive mercy and find grace to help in time of need.* (Heb 4:15 RSV)

    Because of his importunity (persistence?), God will give him what he wants.

DISCIPLESHIP

> *I tell you, though he will not get up and give him anything (bread loaves for an "Out Of Towner") because he is his friend, yet because of his importunity he will rise and give him whatever he needs.* (Luke 11:8 RSV)

- Jesus taught His disciples how to pray.

> *Pray then **like** this:*
> *Our Father who art in heaven,*
> *Hallowed be this name.*
> *Thy kingdom come,*
> *Thy will be done,*
> *On earth as it is in heaven.*
> *Give us this day our daily bread.*
> *And forgive us our debts ("sins"),*
> *As we also have forgiven our debtors.*
> *And lead us not into temptation, But deliver us from evil.* (Matt 6:9–13 RSV)

There are several teaching points here:

- Right off, I noticed in Jesus's teaching His guys on prayer, He said, "Pray then LIKE this." The Lord's Prayer is a template. I do not for a minute think Jesus meant us to say this exact prayer, as like saying a hocus pocus that would be heaping empty phrases. Jesus wanted His guys and all disciples that followed to pray prayers from the heart, from the depths of our souls. I think this should be emphasized in our discipling.
- "Hallowed be thy name" recognizes just how holy His name and His person is. Do we really know how big or important God is?
- "Thy kingdom come, Thy will be done, on earth as it is in heaven" shows submission by the prayer to God. In the middle of the night just before Jesus's very last moments,

Jesus says this by saying, *"And going a little farther, he fell on His face and prayed, 'My Father, if it be possible, let this cup pass from me; nevertheless, not as I will, but as thou wilt'"* (Matt 26:39 RSV). Let this sink in for you and your disciple that **even Jesus** prayed to have this horrible thing that was about to unfold (and He knew how horrible it was going to be). Jesus said basically, "Not my will but THY will be done."

- He asked for just the basics: our daily bread.
- He taught them to ask for forgiveness. Two things here: 1) Jesus did not ask for forgiveness of His sins. He had not sinned. He was teaching, and 2) He used the past tense of forgive by saying, *"As we have forgiven our debtors."* By including this "as we have forgiven our debtors" kind of means, "Before you come to ME, it is kind of assumed you have already forgiven those who have or might sinned against you!" This inclusion is not insignificant!
- He taught them to ask God for help to help keep them from temptation.

There is an element of that prayer that is very, very personal and teaching for me. Four little words: "Thy will be done."

After numerous heart operations, bypasses, replacements of pacemakers, my brother John gave it up and died. BUT not before he taught me a really valuable lesson: put EVERYTHING to the test, the crucible of, can you say, "But not my will, God, but allow, THY will be done"?

In the weeks leading up to his death, John and I would talk or, moments later, text, and he was so anxious that the pain would stop, that the rubber band in his heart would stop snapping him. And yet, in all this, John would ALWAYS add at the end, "Not my will, but THY will be done."

10. ACTS acronym

There is a simple acronym you can follow yourself and teach your disciple(s) that covers all the elements covered by the Lord's

DISCIPLESHIP

Prayer (although Jesus's teaching on prayer was in a little bit different order.)

    A—Adoration
    C—Confession
    T—Thanksgiving
    S—Supplication (Petitioning)

This order is important, but it is not some sort of requirement that it includes every single element. However, every time you pray, it can be a constant reminder to approach God with praise and Thanksgiving and remember who exactly we are talking with and how great He is.

The acronym breaks down as follows:

- *A—Adoration*

    For me, this is the fun part: my chance to tell God how much I love and <u>adore</u> Him for who He is and for all Christ His Son has done. It's also a chance for me to begin by remembering just who it is I am talking <u>with</u>.

    - He created the world (!), and before He did that, He knew MY name. He had plans for ME.
    - He's big—I mean REALLY big. One of my favorite things to think on as I begin a prayer is to think of myself as walking into this throne room. It's huge. It's bigger than a football stadium; it's bigger than a hundred football stadiums. It's bigger than I can imagine. Then I remember: this great God wants <u>more than anything</u> to talk with little old me!
    - One of my disciples described what the experience was for him. For him, it was like walking down this path, kind of through a maze of ten-foot-high bushes, to this quiet place. In the center of this place was a bench and God, and he would sit down and talk.

- Can you see how talking with God may be different for each of you? Find out what it's like for your disciple; it will blow your mind and heart!

- ### *C—Confession*

    God cannot look on sin, so if you've gotten something in there, let it out. Get this out of there; approach God with a clean heart, laying it ALL out there on the table. This clears the blocks between you and God if you are full and truthful with Him. (Might as well lay it out there. He knows it anyway! There is absolutely nothing unknown to Him about you. Scary, huh?)

    Prayers of confession no longer need to be made through a human (or a saintly) intermediary. As pointed out above, because of the work of Christ on the cross, we do not HAVE TO rely on a priest to talk to God. HOWEVER, confessing our sins one to another is useful and helpful. James in his letter writes, _"Therefore_ (remember to go back and see what the "therefore" is there for) _confess your sins to one another, that you may be healed. The prayer of a righteous man has great power in effect"_ (Jas 5:16 RSV).

    Sin, unconfessed to God, flat-out HINDERS any prayer you might offer. It is a blockage, a barrier. Make sure you and your disciples think on this one before offering up any prayer. Enough said.

- ### *T—Thanksgiving*

    This goes back to the A: Adoration, but do you and your disciple always give thanks in all circumstances? We give thanks for the food he provides. Sometimes, we give thanks when we manage to get out of a jam (!) or "Thanks, God, for this beautiful day!" But do we give thanks in all things and situations? This ties back to the concept of "Thy will be done." If we cannot give thanks, we are not acknowledging His purpose for allowing us to this point, His control of the end result; basically, we are not yielding to His sovereignty in our life. Ideally, if we are connected to Christ, we should be able to thank Him when we are hit with insurmountable difficulties! We should rely on His Word and know deep down that He has a plan for you and me AND that He will bring it to conclusion when it meets His timing. We don't have to worry about our particular situation or, on a broader scale, what will happen with the next election and who will rule. I have read the book, and here's a news flash: God wins!

Think on this for a while.

Sometimes, prayer is just a point where you are struck by something only God could bring about, and you just want to thank Him for it. You get this overwhelming desire to stop in your tracks and acknowledge who God is or that God loves you—itty-bitty you—or to remind you that God wants, really WANTS your marriage to work out. It's how He designed us, and God OFTEN is the glue that binds us together

Other times, tough times, we should try (!) and give thanks then as well because we don't know in the moment how God might use that event to do something good!

Thank God in all circumstances for this is the will of God for you in Christ Jesus.

- *S—Supplication (Requests)*

This is the easy part, right? But are we asking rightly or out of selfishness to satisfy our own wants? Also, especially when we are in a tough spot, we put this part of prayer ahead of all the other parts.

If your heart and your life is pretty close to God, the more likely your requests will align with His will. Think on that: the more time you spend with Him, the more likely your thoughts (and requests) are His thoughts.

Ask humbly and earnestly, knowing God hears you and understands you more than you do. Be patient.

Psalm 40:1 RSV says, *"I waited patiently for the Lord, He inclined His ear and heard my cry."*

More often than not, our prayers are often dominated by our requests. You and your coach and you and your disciple should have a hard conversation about this.

11. Prayer lists

Prayer lists are **not** "what I want for Christmas" lists.

In our house, when our kids were growing up, each year we'd have each child come up with and write down a list of things they'd like to get for Christmas and then each gift hoped for had to be rated—as in Kinda Want, Would Like to Have, Gotta Have!—with each request being given a rating one star, two stars, up to about five stars, with five always being, Just Gotta Have!

Prayer lists are lists of things we want to talk to God about, so WE don't forget! If you tell someone, "Hey, I will pray for you," then put it on the list so YOU don't forget. On that thought, if you or your disciple SAY something like, "I will pray for you about _____," be careful to honor that pledge, that covenant; promising to pray for others is not a thing to be casual about carrying out!

Prayer lists might contain an item, an event, or a person that you want to commit to praying for on a regular basis.

Prayer is a conversation with God, and prayer lists can be a tool that could help you not to forget to talk to God about. Example: If I need to talk to my wife, Sue, about several items, things we want to do or buy or just discuss, I can write them down so I don't forget. (This is especially useful when you get older and tend to forget more stuff! LOL.)

- What should we pray or petition for?
    o Others? Surely yes!
    o Outcomes? Not so sure we should do this!
    o Our needs vs. our wants? Jesus asked for His portion of daily bread, sustenance.

- o The government and those in authority. The Bible says (in several places!), "Do it!"
  - 1 Timothy 2:1–4
  - Romans 13:1
  - Philippians 4:6
  - Proverbs 21:1
  - Colossians 1:16–17
- o Our enemies. Biblical basis: Matthew 5:44

12. Additional thoughts and principles to be learned and passed on

In selection of His twelve Disciples and immediately <u>preceding</u> His selection, Jesus went up into the hills and prayed all night! When He came down the next morning, He KNEW who the twelve were. He KNEW who the Father wanted Him to work with.

There is an important discipling concept here, a very important concept. Here's Jesus, who is so closely aligned with His Father. Jesus went up to the hills to pray about who the Father wanted Him to work with. Jesus did NOTHING He did not see the Father doing (Jesus said this). Here's Jesus going up into the hills and spending ALL NIGHT praying about this important matter, as His whole ministry and plan rested on these simple guys!

Do we do this?

Do we pray rigorously before we charge out and disciple men?

Do we travail in prayer over it as Jesus did?

Is prayer even a FACTOR in our discipling plan or before we begin discipling?

It was—for Jesus.

So many times, I see pastors and others put out a general call: "Anyone interested in being a disciple or part of a small group on discipling, show up at the meeting in Room 204 this Sunday at 6:00 p.m."

That just is not biblical!

DISCIPLESHIP

If we are to apply Jesus's teaching and His method, then we should be teaching to the masses (as Jesus did) praying (like a mad man!) for God's leading us to the right guys (as Jesus did).

Then <u>*when*</u> we hear God's leading, we should then go out and <u>*select*</u> those whom God wants us to INVEST our time (as Jesus did).

In practical experience, I have found this to result in my needing to be assertive.

Sometimes, after praying about it and receiving instruction, I need to go to the person, either to be my coach or to be someone I have someone I feel has a kindred heart and I'd like to meet with weekly.

This means I have to get off my butt and go to that person and talk to him. It's risky, it's scary, but sometimes, oftentimes actually, it's worked this way: prayer, much prayer, and me coming out of my comfort zone and talking to the guy.

Secondly, Jesus did NOT put out a general call to the masses—the followers on the fringe; the masses followed Him, and Jesus preached to them, but Jesus did not entrust Himself to them. John 2:24–25 (RSV) records, <u>*"He (Jesus) did not trust Himself to them, because He knew all people and needed no one to bear witness of people, for He knew what was in them."*</u>

So Jesus preached to the masses, taught the masses, but DISCIPLED (after much prayer), invested the in-depth teaching, in just a relatively few men, yet look what has happened in the past two thousand years!

My personal witness/testimony is this: when I was a relatively new Christian, I distinctly remember my first discipler asking me directly, "Gary, do you want help or do you want training?" I chose training.

13. *What prayer is not*

Prayer should **not** be like driving up to the Burger King ordering box and shouting out, "I would like a double cheeseburger with fries and a Coke," and then expecting God to have it ready for you when you get to the pay window. (BTW, when you tithe or put money in the basket, it is not a tip or pay for a good sermon (!) or even to invest in any of the various ministries of the church. This is solely between you and God. Are you going to give up control and let Him guide your stewardship? Yes, it's all about stewardship of whatever GOD gives you. God gave it to you; you didn't earn your ginormous salary. God gave it to you to see how you would handle it. Hmmm.

Neither is approaching the God of the universe and asking Him to wave his magic wand to make <u>all</u> things okay.

Hey, I didn't promise this was going to be pleasant; we just need to do it! By contrast though, at the end of this book are some quotes from a seventeenth century monastic man who, through prayer, lived a life in which he was almost constantly in a state or prayer. He devoted His life to "the practice of the presence of God." It may be useful to read some quotes from this man of prayer.

"To Observe"

"Just a walk in the park!"

Have you ever heard that saying, "Oh, it's just a walk in the park"?

That phrase is an encouragement, meaning: "Hey, friend, this is going to be easy!"

Being a disciple is meant to be, and intended to be, pleasant! (See *Mere Christianity* by C. S. Lewis, pgs., 168–172.)

As Gomer Pyle used to say, "Surprise! Surprise!"

It is not meant to be arduous, like the hundred-mile Badwater Run through Death Valley at 132 degrees!

God wants it to be just a walk in the garden with God.

So then, just what DID Jesus mean when He said, "OBSERVE all that I have COMMANDED you"?

Webster has a number of definitions for the word "observe"; among them are the following

1. To conform one's action or practice to (something, such as a law, rite, or practice) comply with)

2. To inspect or take note of (as in "I observed the geese flying south")
3. To celebrate or solemnize in a customary or accepted way (as in "We observe Independence Day")

I think the first one comes closest to Jesus's word "observe." It's not merely watching something or even ceremoniously observe what He commanded us; it is active.

"Observe" is participatory. It is more on the compliance side. Jesus COMMANDED us to do certain things (only two actually: love God and love your neighbor), and we are to comply with what He commanded us.

"Observe" is a Go! word; it is active. It does not mean you sit on the sidelines and watch or observe what is going on before you; it means you get up and do it!

Deuteronomy has several instructions on what it means to observe what God has commanded us including:

> Observe there all the commands I am giving you today. (Deut 11:8 NIV)

> If you carefully Observe all these commands I am giving you to follow…then. (Deut 11:22 NIV)

"All That I Have 'Commanded' You"

To accomplish this great commission, we need to be "teaching them to observe all I have **commanded** you." From this, we need to examine that phrase, "All I have **commanded** you."

As stated above (several times I believe! LOL), Jesus only gave us two actual commandments and said, "On these two commandments depend (hang) all the law and the prophets." Those two commandments were love God and love your neighbor!

It really is that simple.

Also, it frees us up from trying to live up to all the laws in the Old Testament! What a gift that was alone, as we would fail miserably in trying to obey all of the Old Testament laws!

To back that up, some verses that mention or have reference to doing what Jesus had commanded include:

> If you love me, you will keep my commandments. (John 14:15 RSV)

> If you keep my commandments, you will abide in my love. (John 15:10 RSV)

> This is my commandment, that you love one another as I loved you. Greater love has no man than this, that a man lay down his life for his friends. You are my friends if you do what I command you. (John 15:12–14 RSV)

> This I command you, to love one another. (John 15:17 RSV)

> If you continue in my Word, you are truly my disciples. (John 8:31 RSV)

So in Jesus's words, being a disciple is someone who loves God (totally) and does all he can to love one another. However, as the word "disciple" was commonly used at the time of Jesus, being a disciple clearly meant you were/are always to be in a discipling relationship. In that relationship, you realize a) you are learning and modeling/imitating what you hear and more importantly see in your discipler, and b) that implied in that is the concept that you will carry it forward to <u>your</u> disciples.

DISCIPLESHIP

"AND LO, I AM WITH YOU ALWAYS, TO THE CLOSE OF THE AGE"

This is an almost forgotten, rarely mentioned, and usually overlooked part of the marching order that actually means so much for us today! Some versions translate it to be, "Behold!" I think it means more to us in a very practical way. I think "And lo" means, "And never, <u>ever</u> forget."

The promise to be with us ALWAYS means that this is something we can realize every second of every day.

It can be in our every thought. It is VERY practical and can become part of every moment in our whole life.

Does it sink deep into you that the Spirit of God is with us ALWAYS?

So no matter where we go, we will (or can) run to Him. (Often, I realize He has already gone before me!)

- He is or can be in my real life, which includes business meetings and conversations, if we allow Him to come and be there.
- He is in our marriage. We realized long ago there are three of us in this marriage.
- He is there at every meal.
- He is there when I arise in the morning, sitting there on the couch (or wherever you spend some quiet time with Him), waiting for you, to listen to little old you, and to talk with and to you.

He will be there—always!

What I found interesting recently in writing about Jesus's marching order is that little phrase, "And lo."

In *Webster*, this tiny word is "used to call attention or to express wonder or surprise." Surprisingly, the *Webster Thesaurus* lists a synonym as "Indeed,"

Was Jesus just saying, "By the way" or "Oh yeah, I have one more thought"?

DISCIPLESHIP

Were Jesus's very last words at that Last Supper casual or minor in meaning?

I don't think so.

It was to precede a very important reminder or instruction.

"Hey, guys, take heart (Jesus knew what persecution they were going to face!), I am going to be there with you and be there FOR you always!"

I think Isaiah more properly addressed this continuity in Isaiah 41:10 ESV, *"Fear not, for I am with you. Be not dismayed, for I am your God. I will strengthen you. I will help you. I will uphold you with my righteous hand."*

As Jesus was concluding the dinner, He had to know His guys were scared, so he offered this comfort. He started by saying, "And lo," as if to say, "Don't forget!"

John further expands on this in quoting Jesus who said, *"But the helper, the Holy Spirit, whom the Father will send in my name, he will teach you all things and bring to your remembrance all that I have said to you"* (John 14:26 ESV).

Lately, I have come to think on and realize this concept of Emmanuel or "God with us." God—the God of the whole freaking universe—loved us enough to come down to earth and live with and among us. We don't deserve it; we aren't worthy of it. Yet God came to earth. AND Jesus said, He, and thus God, will be with us ALWAYS! Wow!

That God would think enough of me to promise me He is always with me and I can talk and confide in Him personally anytime, anywhere! Wow! That blows my mind!

He is indeed with us ALWAYS; whether we realize His presence or not, He is there.

A Call to Action

This book calls out for action, a change.

This book hopefully challenges changes in your lives personally.

It should challenge you to seek out until you find someone to offer a hand to help you grow closer to Christ, as that man emulates for you aspects of the Christ.

This book hopefully will see the eyes of pastors in Christian churches to look anew at the true concept of discipling. For a minute, forget how it might work into existing programs. Look anew at Christ and how He worked (purposefully!) in various circumstances, but don't lose the focus: love God, love another, and go make disciples. This should not be a new program but a new focus for the core of every church.

This book has set out:

- An explanation of the word and concept of a disciple, which has its historical roots before Christ; the use by Christ, in terms in common usage of that day, of what it meant to me and worked in me in 1970 and what still works today.
- A simplification of Jesus's only two commands: to love God with everything you've got and then to love one another, sacrificing our lives, time, and hearts for each other, Christian or not!
- A rather lengthy description of every word in Jesus's last marching orders to His guys, His disciples. That Great Commission basically said, "Go!" and the three concepts

that follow make sense only in relation to the word "Go!" as a participle:
- o   Make disciples,
- o   Baptize them, and
- o   Teach them.

Guys, you have all you need to get going.

Pray about it, seek God's guidance, listen to the Holy Spirit, and…

Go!
Go encouraged!
God is already going ahead of you!

Audience

Considerable thought has been given to just who this book is written to help. Who will be the audience? This directly affected how I wrote it, i.e., will the people who read this be men, women, a class, or small group?

To a men's ministry, I would say things a certain way and go over things, providing a basis a history of experience and biblical references. I may not need to do this if I was talking to a pastor or some pastors about what God has taught me about discipleship. However, even pastors need someone in their lives to mentor/coach them and be there to lead them/to emulate. Hmmm. Can an established and ordained pastor be open to changing to biblically based, early church discipleship? Hmmm.

Do I talk to all believing men? I'd like to because I have a deep-seated personal conviction that all men need to be in at least those three crucial mentoring relationships: one where we are investing in newer believers, one where we have a relationship with someone who is not enamored by our presence, and then one where we ourselves are being mentored.

This desire comes partly from scriptural leading and from my own life. The Bible reminds us of that need in Ecclesiastes 4:9–10 when it says, _"Two are better than one, because they have a good reward for their labor. If either of them falls down, one can help the other up. But pity anyone who falls and has no one to help them up"_ (NIV).

But then, is this only to be for men? What about women who see a need for discipling and/or being discipled? Are they to be ignored? No.

And what about husbands and their wives? Can this not apply to them? Is a husband not to disciple his wife, to help her in her walk? Yes.

There is another aspect to this book and its teaching that I believe with all the firmness in my heart. That is, that regardless of the words I choose, God's Spirit will do the work here. I can write eloquently, cleverly, or like an idiot, and I am convinced, God can still do His stuff and change lives!

Although this book or manual could be used for training disciples of any number of secular causes, the Spirit will direct its use, and if it is on track and truly reflects the heart of God on the matter, then I am convinced God can and will use it wherever He sees a need for this cause to be furthered.

It does not matter to me if anyone reading this book remembers me. My only goal is: did it give glory to God?

Bonus: Excerpts from the Practice of the Presence of God

by Brother Lawrence (Spire Books, 1958, 1967 by Revell)

1. Abstracts are from conversations that he had with one or more other brothers and
2. Abstracts from his fifteen letters.

I include excerpts from the book (about $6 on Amazon!) to put it out there as maybe an example of what real closeness could look like, maybe not as a goal, as it then might become a task to get close to Christ. From my readings of his conversations and letters, I saw nothing but joy in the man; what joy the relationship with Christ had brought him on a daily, almost continual conversation, as if Christ were right next to him all the time!

Brother Lawrence was named Nicholas Herman born in 1666, but came to be known as a lay brother at the Carmelites Monastery in Paris and was always known and referred to as Brother Lawrence. His prayer life led him into a constant communication and communion with God. This state enabled him to do things required in his position and do them, but with almost disregard of the task as one that was appointed by God, so he was happy in it, almost ecstatically happy doing menial tasks.

It is an enviable goal; however, he missed the part about <u>making disciples!</u>

DISCIPLESHIP

There is no record other than his writings that he passed on this way of living on to a next generation.

His efforts were to always look inward, cloistered away in a monastery, trying to achieve something like a Buddhist's nirvana, wherein there is "an extinction of desire of individual consciousness or a state of being disregardful (or unconscious) of one's surroundings, concerns, or obligations" (*Webster*: nirvana).

Jesus commands us to "Go (OUT) and make disciples." Brother Lawrence does not consider this activity.

HOWEVER, the following quotes can give us all pause to consider going deeper into this relationship with God in prayer and meditation.

1. *Conversations*

> The value of this book lies in its Christian humility and simplicity. No conceited scholar was Brother Lawrence; theological and doctrinal debates bored him, if he noticed them at all. His one desire was for communion with God. (Ibid, Pg. 11)
>
> Br. Lawrence was a simple man, assigned kitchen duties as a cook and did the clean up as well. By all accounts he was lame and on "business duties." Example: "going to Burgundy (France) to get wine for the Society which was a very unwelcome task for him, because he had no turn (desire) for business, and because he was lame and could not go about the boat but by rolling himself over the casks." (Ibid, Pg. 19)
>
> He took it as God's business that he was about and "gave himself no uneasiness about it." (Ibid, Pg. 19)
>
> Perhaps the greatest men are those who never seek greatness at all, but who personify the virtues which posterity calls great. His one desire

DISCIPLESHIP

was for (Continual) Communion with God. (Ibid, Preface, Pg. 11, Emphasis added)

From that moment on (being accepted into the Carmelites) he grew and waxed strong in the knowledge and love and favor of God, endeavoring constantly, as he put it, "to walk as in His presence." (Ibid, Pg. 12)

A wholly consecrated man, he lived his life as though he were a singing Pilgrim on the march, as happy in serving his fellow monks and brothers from the monastery kitchen as in serving God in the vigil of prayer and penance. (Ibid, Pgs. 12–13)

He showed us how, at any moment and in any circumstance, the soul that seeks God may find Him, and practice the presence of God. (Ibid, Pg. 13)

That we should establish ourselves in a sense of God's presence by continually conversing with Him. That it was a shameful thing to quit his conversation to think of trifles and fooleries. (Ibid, Pg. 16)

That we ought to give ourselves up to God, with regard to things temporal and spiritual and seek our satisfaction only in fulfilling of His will, whether He leads us by suffering or consolation, for all would be equal to a soul truly resigned. (Ibid, Pg. 16)

That to arrive at such resignation as God requires, we should watch attentively over all the passions which mingle as well in spiritual things as in those of a grosser nature; that God would give light concerning those passions to those who truly desire to serve Him. (Ibid, Pg. 17)

That having resolved to make the love of God the _end_ of all his actions, he had found reason to be well satisfied with his method. (Ibid, Pg. 17)

That in order to for a habit of conversing with God continually, and referring all we do to Him, we must first apply **to** Him with some diligence; but after a little care we should find His love inwardly excite us to it without any difficulty. (Ibid, Pg. 18)

That we ought to act with God in the greatest simplicity, speaking to Him frankly and plainly, and imploring His assistance in our affairs, just as they happen. (Ibid, Pg. 19)

He was very pleased with the post he was now in, but that he was as ready to quit that as the former, since he was always pleasing to himself in every condition by doing little things for the love of God. (Ibid, Pg. 20)

Useless thoughts spoil all, that the mischief began there but that we ought to reject them as soon as we perceive their impertinence to the matter in hand…and return to our communion with God. (Ibid, Pg. 21)

That we ought to make a great difference between the acts of the understanding and those of the will; that the first were comparatively of little value, and the others, all. (Ibid, Pg. 21)

That God seemed to have granted the greatest favors to the greatest sinners, as more signal monuments of His mercy. (Ibid, Pg. 22)

When sometimes he had not thought of God for a good while, he did not disgust himself for it; but, after having acknowledged his wretchedness to God, he returned to Him with so much the greater trust in Him as he found himself wretched through forgetting Him. (Ibid, Pg. 23)

In the beginning of the spiritual life, we ought to be faithful in doing our duty and denying ourselves; but after that, unspeakable pleasures followed. (Ibid, Pg. 24)

Many do not advance in the Christian progress because they stick in penances and particular exercises, while they neglect the Love of God, which is the ***end***. (Ibid, Pg. 24)

He told me that all consists in one hearty renunciation of everything which we are sensible does not lead to God. That we might accustom ourselves to a continual conversation with Him, with freedom and simplicity. (Ibid, Pg. 25)

That the most excellent method he had found of going to God was that of doing our common business without any view of pleasing men. (Gal 1:10 and Eph 6:5, 6) and (as far as possible) purely for the love of God. That it was a great delusion to think that the times of prayer ought to differ from other times. (Ibid, Pg. 26)

That we ought to be weary of doing little things for the love of God, who regards not the greatness of the work, but the love with which is performed. (Ibid, Pg. 27)

That the end we ought to propose to ourselves is to become, in this life, the most perfect worshipers of God we can possibly be, as we hope to be through all eternity. (Ibid, Pg. 27)

2. *Letters*

Having found in many books different methods of going to God, and divers practices of the spiritual life, I thought this would serve rather to puzzle me than facilitate what I sought after, which was nothing but how to become wholly God's. (Ibid, Pg. 31)

I found no small pain in this exercise, and yet I continued it notwithstanding all the difficulties that occurred without troubling or disquieting myself when my mind had wandered involuntarily. (Ibid, Pg. 32)

Ever since that time I walked before God, simply, in faith, with humility and with love, and I apply myself diligently to do nothing and think nothing which may displease Him. I hope that when I have done what I can, He will do with me what He pleases. (Ibid, Pg. 35)

And I make it my business only to persevere in His presence, wherein I keep myself by a simple attention, and a general fond regard to God, or, to speak better, an habitual, silent, and secret conversation of the soul with God, which often causes me joys and raptures inwardly, and sometimes also outwardly, so great that I am forced to use means to moderate them and prevent their appearance to others. (Ibid, Pg. 36)

The King, full of mercy and goodness, very far from chastising me, embraces me with love, makes me eat at His table, serves me with His own hands, gives me the key of His treasures; He converses and delights Himself with me incessantly, in a thousand and a thousand ways, and treats me in all respects as His favorite. It is thus I consider myself from time to time in His Holy presence. (Ibid, Pg. 37)

I should choose to call this state the bosom of God, for the inexpressible sweetness which I taste and experience there. (Ibid, Pg. 37)

Sometimes I consider myself as a stone before a carver, whereof He is to make a statue;

presenting myself thus before God, I desire Him to form His perfect image in my soul, and make me entirely like Himself. (Ibid, Pg. 37)

A little remembrance of God, one act of inward worship, though upon a march, and a sword in hand, are prayers, which, however short, are nevertheless very acceptable to God... No one will notice it, and nothing is easier than to repeat often in the day these little adorations. (Ibid, Pg. 39)

You must know his continual care has been, for about 40 years past, that he has spent in religion (monastic life) to be always with God, and to do nothing, say nothing, and think nothing which may displease Him, and without any other view than purely for the love of Him, and because He deserves infinitely more. (Ibid, Pg. 40)

There is not in the world a kind of life more sweet and delightful than that of a continual conversation with God...but let us do it from a principle of love, and because God would have us. (Ibid, Pg. 44)

We must serve God in a holy freedom; we must do our business faithfully, without trouble or disquiet. Recalling our mind to God mildly, and with tranquility, as often as we find it wandering. (Ibid, Pg. 46)

You need not cry very loud; He is nearer to us than we are aware of. (Ibid, Pg. 47)

I believe one remedy for this (wandering thoughts in prayer) is to confess our faults and to humble ourselves before God. I do not advise you use multiplicity of words in prayer—many words and long discourses being often the occasions of wandering. Hold yourself before God like a dumb or paralytic beggar at a rich man's gate. (Ibid, Pg. 49)

One does not become holy all at once. (Ibid, Pg. 50)

Let us renounce, let us generously renounce, for the love of Him, all that is not Himself; He deserves infinitely more. Let us think of Him perpetually. Let us put all our trust in Him. (Ibid, Pg. 51)

We cannot have too much in so good and faithful a Friend, who will never fail us in this world, nor in the next. (Ibid, Pg. 52)

You would think it rude to leave a friend alone who came to visit you; why then must God be neglected? Do not forget Him, but think on Him often, adore Him continually, live and die with Him. (Ibid, Pg. 52)

I know not how God will dispose of me. I am always happy. All the world suffers; and I, who deserve the severest discipline, feel joys so continual and so great that I can scarce contain them. (Ibid, Pg. 56)

Ask God, not deliverance from your pains, but strength to bear resolutely, for the love of Him, all that He should believe, and as long as He shall please. (Ibid, Pg. 57)

Brother Lawrence took to his bed two days after writing this, and he died within one week.

This kind of a life, in my mind, is not the end. Making disciples is what Jesus told us to do. However, it shows an aim of what joy can be found in living a life fully, fully devoted to living in Christ's presence full-time, 24-7.

Resources / References / Recommended Readings

Many of these are quoted in the book. Most of these, I have read and absorbed as they went toward forging who I am today and how I got here.

- Sources: books I have used and/or quoted from.
- Discipleship: books on the topic of discipleship.
- Men's Issues: issues and how to handle them for men.
- Reference: books helpful in understanding difficult issues and sources for research.
- Studies for individuals or small groups.
- Additional Recommended Reading.

Sources

Brother Lawrence. 1958. *The Practice of the Presence of God with Spiritual Maxims.* Spire Books.

Coleman, Robert E. 1970. *The Master Plan of Evangelism.* Old Tappan New Jersey: Fleming H. Revell Company.

God. *Holy Bible.* My version RSV. Translated from the original tongues. Being the version set forth in AD 1611, revised AD 1881–1885 and AD 1901 Published by Concordia Publishing House, St. Louis MO, 1952. Also used NIV as well as NASB translations as they sometimes translated the verse(s) into more relatable or understandable versions.

Lewis, C. S. 1963. *Mere Christianity.* Simon and Schuster.

Lewis, C. S. 1963. *The World's Last Night and Other Essays.* A Harvest, HBJ (Harcourt Brace Jovanovich Publishers) Book

Schaeffer, Francis A. 1970. *The Mark of the Christian.* Downers Grove IL: InterVarsity Press.

Stanford, Miles J. 1966. *Principals of Spiritual Growth.* Back to the Bible Broadcast.

Stott, John R. W. 1995. *Basic Christianity.* Grand Rapids MI: William B. Eerdmans Publishing Company.

Discipleship

(12 Inductive Studies for Neighborhood, Student, and Church Groups)

1980. *Design for Discipleship.* Colorado Springs CO: NavPress.

Bonhoeffer, Dietrich. 1937. *The Cost of Discipleship.* Simon & Schuster Publishing.

Briscoe, Stuart. 1988. *Discipleship for Ordinary People.* Wheaton IL: Harold Shaw Publishers.

Coleman, Robert E. 1987, repackaged and edition published 2020. *The Master Plan of Discipleship.* Grand Rapids, MI: Revell Company, a Division of Baker Publishing Group. www.revell-books.com.

Cosgrove, Francis M., Jr. 1980. *Essentials of Discipleship: Practical Help on How to Live as Christ's Disciple.* NavPress.

Foster, Richard J. 1988. *Celebration of Discipline: The Path to Spiritual Growth.* San Francisco CA: Harper Collins Publishers.

Harrington, Bobby, and Alex Hamilton. 2016. *Discipleship That Fits: The Five Kinds of Relationships God Uses to Help Us Grow.* Zondervan.

Hull, Bill. 2006. *The Complete Book of Discipleship: On Being and Making Followers of Christ.* NavPress.

(A Discipleship.Org Resource)

Ogden, Greg. 2016. *Transforming Discipleship: Making Disciples a Few at a Time.* InterVarsity Press.

Putnam, Jim and Bobby Harrington, with Robert E. Coleman. *Disciple-Shift: Five Steps That Help Your Church to Make Disciples Who Make Disciples.*
Rainer, Thom S. and Eric Geiger. 2011. *Simple Church: Returning to God's Process for Making Disciples.* Nashville TN: B&H Publishing Group.
Reapsome, James and Martha Reapsome. *Discipleship: The Growing Christians Lifestyle.* Wheaton IL: Harold Shaw Publishers.
Watson, David. 1982. *Called and Committed: World Changing Discipleship.* Wheaton IL: Harold Shaw Publishers.
Whitney, Donald S. Foreword by J. J. Packer. 1991. *Spiritual Disciplines for the Christian Life.* Colorado Springs CO: NavPress.
(Small Group Bible Study)
Wilkins, Michael J. 1992. *Following the Master: A Biblical Theology of Discipleship.* Grand Rapids MI: Zondervan Publishing House.

Men's Issues

Arterburn, Stephen, Fred Stoeker with Mike Yorkey. 2004. *Every Man's Challenge: How Far Are You Willing to Go for God?* Waterbrook Press.
Dabbs, Reggie with John Driver. 2010. *Reggie: You Can't Change Your Past, But You Can Change Your Future.* Nashville TN: Thomas Nelson, Inc.
Dobson, James, Gary Smalley, Tony Evans, Bill McCartney, Luis Palau, and others. 1999. *Seven Promises of a Promise Keeper.* Thomas Nelson, Inc.
Farrar, Steve. 1990. *Point Man: How a Man Can Lead His Family* (Includes a Study Guide). Multnomah Books.
Hughes, R. Kent. 2001. *Disciplines of a Godly Man.* Crossway.
Kasich, John. 2010. *Every Other Monday: Twenty Years of Life, Lunch, Faith, and Friendship.* Atria Books: A Division of Simon and Schuster.
Lewis, Greg. 1993. *The Power of a Promise Kept: Life Stories.* Focus on the Family Publishing.

Morley, Patrick M. 1997. *The Man in the Mirror: Solving the 24 Problems Man Face.* Zondervan Publishing House.

Oliver, Gary J. PhD. 1993. *Men of Integrity: Real Men Have Feelings Too.* Chicago IL: Moody Press.

Promise Keepers. 1996. *Man of His Word.* Colorado Springs CO: International Bible Society.

(A gift to me from my son, Travis Z. Beisheim, on 6/19/1994)

Swindoll, Charles R. 1981. *Improving Your Serve: The Art of Unselfish Living.* Word Publishing.

Tome, Brian. 2018. *The Five Marks of a Man: Finding Your Path to Courageous Manhood.* Grand Rapids MI: Baker Books.

Knowing the Will of God for Your Life

Maeder, Gary. 1973. *God's Will for Your Life: How God Wants You to Live in the World Today: An Easy-to-Use Biblical Guide.* Wheaton IL: Tyndale House Publishers, Inc.

Packer, J.I. 1995. *Knowing and Doing the Will of God: Daily Devotions.* Vine Books, an imprint of Servant Publications.

Riggs, Charlie. 1988. *Learning to Walk with God.* World Wide Publications.

Sanders, J. Oswald. 1984. *Every Life Is a Plan of God: Discovering His Will for Your Life.* Discovery House Publishers.

Stark, Tom and Joan Stark. 1978. *Guidance and God's Will (11 Studies for Individuals or Groups).* Wheaton IL: Harold Shaw Publishers.

Warren, Rick. 2002. *The Purpose Drive Life: What on Earth Am I Here For?* Zondervan.

Reference

1987. *Smith's Bible Dictionary.* Uhrichsville OH: Barbour and Company, Inc. 2005. *Rose Book of Bible Charts, Maps and Time Lines 10th Anniversary Edition.* Rose Publishing. Printed by Regent Publishing Services, Ltd.

Haley's Bible Handbook. Zondervan Publishing House, A Division of Harper Collins Publishers.

Alexander, David and Pat Alexander. 1981. *The Lion Handbook to the Bible.* Lion Publishing (color illustrated for each book and section of the Bible).

Arthur, Kay. 1994. *How to Study Your Bible: Precept upon Precept.* Eugene, OR: Harvest House Publishers.

Canne, Browne, Blaney, Scott, and Others. 1967. *Treasury of Scripture Knowledge: Five Hundred Thousand Scripture References and Parallel Passages.* Fleming H. Revell Company. (Copy given to me by Lt. Mike Welch on the occasion of my twentieth birthday, January 12, 1970.)

Dillard, Raymond B. and Tremper Longman III. 1993. *An Introduction to the Old Testament.* Grand Rapids, MI: Zondervan Publishing House.

Douglas, J. D. and Merrill C. Tenney. 1993. *New Compact Dictionary of the Bible.* Zondervan Publishing House.

Jones, D. Martin Lloyd. 1958. *Authority.* Chicago, IL: InterVarsity Press. McDowell, Josh. 1999. *The New Evidence That Demands a Verdict* (Evidence I & II). Published by Here's Life Publishing.

Nave, Orville J. *Nave's Topical Bible: Condensed Edition.* Chicago: Moody Press.

Richards, I. A. 1964. *Why So Socrates?* Cambridge University Press.

Stalker, James. *Life of Christ.* Barbour and Company, Inc. (Publisher).

Sanders, E. P. 1993. *The Historical Figure of Jesus.* Allen Lane / The Penguin Press.

Sproul, R. C. 1977. *Knowing Scripture.* Downers Grove IL: Intervarsity Press.

Torrey, R. A. *Difficulties in the Bible: Alleged Errors and Contradictions.* Chicago, IL: Moody Press.

Additional Recommended Reading

1993. Edited with commentary by William J. Bennett. *The Book of Virtues: A Treasury of Great Moral Stories.* Simon and Schuster.

1997. *Just As I Am: The Autobiography of Billy Graham.* New York, NY: Harper Collins Publishers.

Bonhoeffer, Dietrich. 1995. *Ethics.* Simon and Schuster.

Buckingham, Jamie. 1983. *Power for Living.* Arthur S. DeMoss Foundation.

Buscaglia, Leo, PhD. 1982. *Living, Loving, and Learning.* Charles B. Slack, Inc. Eyre, Stephen D. 1995. *Drawing Close to God: Essentials of a Dynamic Quiet Time.* Downers Grove, IL: InterVarsity Press.

Graham, Billy. 1968. *Peace with God.* Old Tappan, NJ: Spier Books.

King, Martin Luther Jr. 1963. *Strength to Love.* New York, NY: Harper and Row. Republished by Pocket Books.

Packer, J. I. 1973. *Knowing God.* InterVarsity Press.

Small Group Studies

The following are some great small group studies from six-, nine- and thirteen-week studies to thirty- and thirty-one-day transformations and Ogden's thirty-week course.

These are not added to help you get more educated/knowledgeable but rather to help you get the basics and more importantly, biblically based studies that help you get connected to others in the group so you can bond and come alongside another young believer.

1980. *Growing in Christ: A Thirteen-Week Follow-Up Course for New and Growing Christians.* Colorado Springs, CO: NavPress.

1984. *Beginning a Men's Group: Six Sessions on Men's Issues.* International Bible Society.

Baker, Donald. 2001. *Decisions: Seeking God's Guidance (Nine Studies for Individuals or Groups).* Downers Grove, IL: InterVarsity Press.

Compiled by Deena Davis. 2005. *Best Small-Group Ideas.* Colorado Springs, CO: NavPress.

Gorsuch, Geoff with Dan Schaffer. 1994. *Brothers! Calling Men into Vital Relationships (A Small Group Discussion Guide).* NavPress.

Hybels, Bill. 1994. *Who You Are When No One's Looking: Six Studies for Individuals or Groups.* Downers Grove, IL: InterVarsity Press.

Nyquist, James F. and James Kuhatschek. 1985. *Leading Bible Discussions.* InterVarsity Press.

Peel, William Carr. 1993. *What God Does When Men Pray: A Small Group Discussion Guide.* NavPress.

Purnell, Dick. 1985. *Thirty-One-Day Experiment.* San Bernadino, CA: Here's Life Publishing.

Stott, John. 1994. *God's Word for Contemporary Christians: Six Studies for Individuals or Groups.* Downers Grove, IL: InterVarsity Press.

Vujivic, Nick. 2020. *Jesus Is the Answer: Thirty Days to a Transformed Life.* Life without Limits.

About the Author

Gary Beisheim has retired as a forensic accountant for the FBI but continues his work and passion (which began in 1970) to disciple others, helping them develop their relationship to Jesus Christ. Although he was ordained as an elder in a former church, today he is a layperson in the church, working with guys in the church and with friends he developed through his work.

www.ingramcontent.com/pod-product-compliance
Lightning Source LLC
Jackson TN
JSHW020907110525
84152JS00001B/42